Cambridge Elements ≡

Elements in Creativity and Imagination
edited by
Anna Abraham
University of Georgia, USA

NARRATIVE CREATIVITY

An Introduction to How and Why

Angus Fletcher
Ohio State University

Mike Benveniste
Ohio State University

CAMBRIDGE
UNIVERSITY PRESS

Shaftesbury Road, Cambridge CB2 8EA, United Kingdom

One Liberty Plaza, 20th Floor, New York, NY 10006, USA

477 Williamstown Road, Port Melbourne, VIC 3207, Australia

314–321, 3rd Floor, Plot 3, Splendor Forum, Jasola District Centre, New Delhi – 110025, India

103 Penang Road, #05–06/07, Visioncrest Commercial, Singapore 238467

Cambridge University Press is part of Cambridge University Press & Assessment, a department of the University of Cambridge.

We share the University's mission to contribute to society through the pursuit of education, learning and research at the highest international levels of excellence.

www.cambridge.org
Information on this title: www.cambridge.org/9781009614788

DOI: 10.1017/9781009614801

First published 2025

A catalogue record for this publication is available from the British Library

ISBN 978-1-009-61478-8 Hardback
ISBN 978-1-009-61477-1 Paperback
ISSN 2752-3950 (online)
ISSN 2752-3942 (print)

Cambridge University Press & Assessment has no responsibility for the persistence or accuracy of URLs for external or third-party internet websites referred to in this publication and does not guarantee that any content on such websites is, or will remain, accurate or appropriate.

Narrative Creativity

An Introduction to How and Why

Elements in Creativity and Imagination

DOI: 10.1017/9781009614801
First published online: January 2025

Angus Fletcher
Ohio State University

Mike Benveniste
Ohio State University

Author for correspondence: Angus Fletcher, fletcher.300@osu.edu

Abstract: Narrative creativity is a new, neuroscience-based approach to innovation, problem solving, and resilience that has proved effective in business executives, scientists, engineers, doctors, and students as young as eight. This Element offers a concise introduction to narrative creativity's theory and practice. It distinguishes narrative creativity from ideation, divergent thinking, design thinking, brainstorming, and other current approaches to cultivating creativity. It traces the biological origins of narrative creativity and explains why narrative creativity will always be mechanically impossible for computer artificial intelligences. It provides practical exercises, developed and tested in hundreds of classrooms and businesses, and validated independently by the US Army, for improving narrative creativity. It explains how narrative creativity contributes to technological innovation, scientific progress, cultural growth, and psychological well-being, and it describes how narrative creativity can be assessed. This title is also available as Open Access on Cambridge Core.

Keywords: creativity, innovation, narrative, neuroscience, artificial intelligence

ISBNs: 9781009614788 (HB), 9781009614771 (PB), 9781009614801 (OC)
ISSNs: 2752-3950 (online), 2752-3942 (print)

Contents

1 Why Read This Book?

School. It's meant to equip us for life. But life requires creativity. And school is failing to cultivate creativity. In fact, school may be *decreasing* it.

This book will try to change that. It will outline the limitations of current approaches to teaching creativity. And it will lay out new creativity training for students of all levels, from third grade through MBA. So, if you're a teacher, you can help your students grow their creative potential. And if you're a student, you can reach it.

1.1 Creativity: And Why It Matters

Creativity is for artists. And also for engineers, scientists, nurses, doctors, entrepreneurs, leaders, administrators, soldiers, managers, teachers, coaches, athletes, gardeners, chefs, parents, and *everyone*.

That's because creativity solves new problems, provides better answers to old problems, and enriches life with fresh opportunities. This practical, real-world power is the reason that creativity is consistently listed by global agencies such as UNESCO and the World Economic Forum as a top priority of international governments and employers.[1]

By helping us overcome challenges and maximize possibilities, creativity strengthens mental well-being. It elevates optimism, making us believe that we *can*. It stirs courage, inspiring us to try new things. And it feeds resilience, giving us more bounce-back when we fail, so that instead of getting discouraged or angry, we treat setback as a chance to find a different way.

Which is why we should be concerned about what's happening in school today.

1.2 The Decrease of Creativity at School

For decades, researchers have observed a decline in students' performance on creative tasks.[2] The decline starts around third grade and persists for as long as students remain in school.[3] It continues in college and in graduate programs.[4] It is not reversed by coursework in engineering, design, and other fields that emphasize innovation and creative problem-solving.[5]

---

[1] Florida 2006; Lee et al. 2010; Pellegrino and Hilton 2012; "'The Skills Needed in the 21st Century – New Vision for Education' from New Vision for Education: Fostering Social and Emotional Learning through Technology." 2015; "Education Must Foster Creativity – and Fight Inequality" 2017; Center for the New Economy and Society 2018, 2020, 2023; Florida 2019.

[2] Land and Jarman 1993; Kyung Hee Kim 2011; Kim 2016; Henriksen et al. 2019.

[3] Torrance 1967; Barbot et al. 2016; Hui et al. 2019.

[4] Cheung et al. 2003; Genco et al. 2012; Sola et al. 2017; Coleman et al. 2020.

[5] Cropley 2015; Surovek and Rassati 2017; Belski and Belski 2018; Valentine et al. 2018; Valentine et al. 2019.

If you graduate with a PhD in Computer Science, an MEd, an MBA, a medical degree, or even an MFA, you will be less creative than you were in preschool. You'll be more of an expert in your field, but you'll have less ability to solve the big problems or initiate the deep changes necessary to improve computers, education, business, medicine, and art.

The decline in student creativity has been accompanied by a drop in resilience, meaning that when students are confronted with hard problems, they are more likely to:

- give up;
- get aggressive, trying to brute force problems;
- look to authority figures for help.

This has led to decreases in self-efficacy, the belief that we can accomplish our goals. And it has also led to increases in anxiety, anger, dissociation, and magical thinking.[6] (Magical thinking is when creativity detaches from reality, leading us to skip over laws of physics and psychology, so that instead of coming up with answers that we can practically test, we pivot into fantasy, daydreaming that we're a superhero or a wizard.)

The net result is that students are struggling not just to solve the world's problems but to handle their own. They're losing faith in their practical competence, becoming less confident and self-reliant. They're getting better at standardized tests and worse at life.

This situation is, however, ours to change.

1.3 What This Book Will Do For You

This book offers a new approach to training creativity, an approach rooted in neuroscience and narrative theory.

Narrative theory has never previously been applied to creativity training,[7] so this book will describe what narrative theory is and why it can be useful at improving our brain's performance at solving problems and generating innovations. It will explain that we've been miseducated to see narrative as a product of creativity, when, in fact, narrative is an engine of creativity. Narrative is what our brain uses to invent new plans, new tools, and new ways of doing.

This book will also show that we've been miseducated to think that narrative is made of language, themes, representations, and meanings. Language, themes, representations, and meanings are elements of symbolic logic, which is a tool for computing equations such as *2 + 2 = 4* and *peace is good*. Symbolic logic

---

[6] Pennequin et al. 2020.   [7] Fletcher and Benveniste 2022.

can run induction, deduction, interpretation, and Bayesian statistics, but it cannot run narrative. Narrative is constituted from actions; actions contain causes; and as logicians from Aristotle to Bertrand Russell have demonstrated, symbolic logic can compute correlations, but it cannot discover the mechanical workings of causes.

The most evident causes in narratives are characters. Characters are actors. They initiate actions. But narratives contain many other causes, including:

- *Motives*, the psychological forces that prompt characters to act as they do.
- *Plots*, chains or branching sequences of actions, all of which cause other actions, both in the story and in the audience's mind.
- *Storyworlds*, the rules that govern what can happen in a given narrative.
- *Narrators*, the ultimate cause of any narrative, the deep *why* beneath its operations.

Narrative theory reveals the mechanics of these causes, enabling us to grow and focus our brain's natural ability to generate original sequences of actions, aka, behaviors, plans, and strategies. The more diverse our behaviors, plans, and strategies, the more effectively we can react to challenges and opportunities, improving resilience, innovation, and leadership.

To translate narrative theory into practice, the following sections will outline narrative techniques for boosting creativity. Basic techniques include causal and counterfactual thinking. (That is, speculating *why* and *what if?*) More advanced techniques include spotting exceptional information, leveraging conflict, matching volatility, and performing process recognition.

These techniques will be illustrated in Sections 8 and 9 via sample exercises for students from third grade through executive MBA. The exercises are not hypothetical. They have been run in hundreds of classrooms, and they have been shown in scientific trials to increase creative problem-solving, major innovation, self-efficacy, and resilience in students as young as eight.

Along the way, this book will touch on the origins of narrative creativity in ancient art across the globe. And by drawing on the authors' years of academic and commercial research in natural language processors and other artificial intelligences, including current generation large language models (LLMs), it will explain why computers will never be capable of narrative creativity. The path to a more innovative and resilient future won't be invented by data and algorithms. It requires theater, literature, and human intelligence.

But first, to set the stage for this book's new approach, the next section will describe the current approach to training creativity.

2 Current Creativity Training

Current creativity training focuses on a pair of computational processes: randomness and symbolic logic.[8] (Symbolic logic will, from here on, be referred to simply as *logic*.)

Randomness and logic can generate semantic and visual variance, which is why AI is able to generate new word patterns and image blends. Such creations can be useful, but they account for a fraction of real-world innovation and problem-solving. By focusing on randomness and logic, current creativity training thus makes us marginally better at creative tasks that we could outsource to AI while neglecting creative tasks that only our brain can do.[9]

To understand how we got here, let's turn back to the beginnings of modern creativity training, eighty years ago.

2.1 The Beginnings of Modern Creativity Training

Modern creativity training traces its origins to American psychologist J. P. Guilford. Guilford worked as an education professor at the University of Southern California from 1940–1962, taking leave during World War II to serve in the US Army Air Force.

When Guilford entered the Army, programs existed for instructing students in math and writing, but there was no effective method for training creativity. In fact, most educators had resigned themselves to the view that creativity was beyond teaching. Unlike algebra and grammar, it was treated as a mysterious mental power, intangible in its origins and operations.

This, to Guilford, was superstition, a holdover of the magical view that human intelligence was driven by immaterial essences. If math and writing could be taught, then so could creativity.[10] It was simply a matter of distilling creativity to physical operations that could be strengthened through practice. Intrigued by Guilford's certainty, the US Army provided him with a lab to crack the secret of creativity. And remarkably, Guilford succeeded – or so at least it seemed. He devised a theory of creativity that inspired modern creativity studies, becoming the core of design thinking, generative AI, and the methods now used to train innovation in twenty-first-century schools and businesses.[11]

Guilford's theory was that creativity could be reduced to randomness and logic.[12]

---

[8] Guilford 1956; Mednick 1962; Dietrich 2004; Mekern, Hommel et al. 2019; Mekern, Sjoerds et al. 2019; Zhang et al. 2020; Runco 2023, chapter 5.

[9] Brucks and Huang 2020; Gonthier and Besançon 2022.   [10] Guilford 1950.

[11] Michael 1999; Bycroft 2012; Van Eekelen 2017.   [12] Guilford 1967, 1968.

Guilford wasn't the first scholar to emphasize the generative power of logic. After the twelfth-century rediscovery of Aristotle's complete *Organon*, logic had become the foundation of European medieval science and its intellectual creations.[13] During the seventeenth- and eighteenth-century Enlightenment, philosophers such as Rene Descartes, Thomas Hobbes, and Immanuel Kant had anatomized technological innovations, artistic imaginations, and other feats of human invention into algorithmic formulas.[14] And in the early twentieth century, psychometricians such as Charles Spearman had concluded that all acts of genius, including creativity, were rooted in a "general intelligence factor" that could be quantified via logical assessments such as IQ.[15]

Nor was Guilford the first to position randomness as a contributor to creativity. The ancient materialist Lucretius had argued that the world was a haphazard creation,[16] and following the synthesis of Darwinism and genetics in the 1930s, modern biologists had credited arbitrary mutation as a component of evolution.[17] Within twentieth-century educational theory, meanwhile, creativity was associated with play, a spontaneous inventiveness hypothesized to drive childhood games, improv performance, jazz music, and even theoretical physics.[18]

Yet although Guilford's basic approach had many antecedents, it achieved its own special impact by capitalizing on a new technology: the computer. In 1943, the same year that Guilford started at his Army lab, the Army began constructing ENIAC, the world's first programmable, electronic, general-purpose computer.[19] ENIAC was built as a logic processor; its primary purpose was to run logical-arithmetic functions such as addition, multiplication, and square roots. But as John von Neumann demonstrated in 1949, ENIAC could also generate random numbers.[20]

ENIAC's mechanization of logic and randomness led Guilford to propose that all creativity was computational. Every human innovation – from the pyramids of Giza, to the plays of Shakespeare, to the invention of the computer itself – had been achieved via the processes that hummed inside the Army's electric machine.

This account of creativity had three revolutionary upshots. The first was that imagination was really *ideation*, the computational generation of new ideas. The second was that people could improve their creativity via training in ideation. The third was that automated ideation, aka computer Artificial Intelligence, would eventually replace human creatives.

---

[13] Swanson 1999. [14] Engell 1981; Nickles 1994. [15] Spearman 1920, 1930.

[16] Greenblatt 2012. [17] Mayr 1993; Huxley 2009. [18] Millar 1968.

[19] Campbell-Kelly et al. 2013.

[20] Von Neumann 1963. For the continued centrality of randomness in computation, see Rahnamayan et al. 2008; Misra et al. 2023; Deng and Lin 2000; Zenil 2011.

Guilford's theory has been expanded and revised over the past six decades by a vast amount of research. But his computational model of idea generation remains the basis of modern creativity training. To understand both the power and the limits of that training, let's delve into the workings of ideation, exploring how it uses logic and randomness to compute new ideas.

2.2 Ideation: Its Major Logical Processes

Computers run all their "general computing" functions on an ALU, or arithmetic logic unit, composed of logic gates. The gates come in different forms, including NAND, NOR, XOR, and XNOR. But they all have the same root function: to execute the triad of logical operations – AND/OR/NOT – that (as Aristotle proved in his *Organon*) constitute the entirety of logic.[21]

Logic can be applied to creativity in different ways,[22] but the three most influential are analogical thinking,[23] design thinking,[24] and convergent thinking.[25]

Analogical Thinking. Start with two objects. Any two will do. A duck and a human. A clock and a business. The American Revolution and your next dinner party.

Hold the objects side-by-side in your mind, comparing their structure. When you do this, you will start to notice similarities. Or, to be technical, your brain will engage in *pattern recognition* (what an algorithm does when it identifies the similarities between a million photographs of canines, abstracting those similarities into the general idea of *dog*).

Once you've abstracted that pattern, you can use it to transfer properties from one object to the other. (For example, you can transfer the duck's webbed foot to the human, the clock's mainspring to the business, and the Revolution's timeline to your dinner party.) The transfer will yield new ideas, enriching the second object with properties from the first. (To continue our example, the new ideas might be a foot-flipper for swimmers, a scheduling app to keep employees operating in clockwork, and a Boston-tea hors d'oeuvre.)

If those ideas don't work for you, look for other patterns – or select other objects. The process can be reiterated endlessly.

Design Thinking. Design thinking is a logical method for inventing products and processes (see Figure 1).

---

[21] Nahin 2017.   [22] Runco and Jaeger 2012.

[23] Mednick 1962; Benedek and Neubauer 2013; Mumford and Martin 2020; Russ and Hoffmann 2020; Runco 2023.

[24] Brown and Katz 2011; Kolko 2014; Brown 2019.   [25] Mumford 2001; Runco 2020.

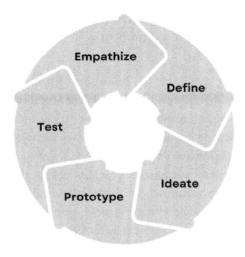

Figure 1 Design thinking.

Step 1: Empathize. Identify your ideal customer or typical user. Observe how they act and deduce what they want, need, and expect. Determine how "customer engagement" or "user experience" is degraded by the problems (or "pain points") posed by current products. Calculate how customer engagement or user experience could be enhanced via innovations.

Step 2: Define. Precisely delineate the problem you are trying to solve or the innovation you are trying to achieve. Do not try to accomplish everything that any customer or user might want. Do not seek an abstract ideal of "improvement." Focus your mind on a single outcome, so that you can target your thinking and clearly assess your progress.

Step 3: Ideate. Generate ideas for how to achieve your defined outcome. You can do so via analogical thinking or other computational processes, such as brainstorming and divergent thinking (see below). Once you have a collection of promising ideas, select your best idea via convergent thinking (see below).

Step 4: Prototype. Convert your idea into a cheap, working product. Build only as much of the product as you need to assess whether your idea accomplishes your defined outcome.

Step 5: Test. Run experimental trials with customer and user groups to measure how effectively your prototype solves your defined problem or achieves your defined innovation. Based on feedback, reiterate Steps 1 through 5, refining and optimizing.

This five-step sequence is itself the product of design thinking: It has been tested and refined by generations of designers to achieve optimum efficiency and results.

Convergent Thinking. Logic can do more than generate ideas. Logic can winnow ideas, selecting the best ones. The winnowing makes ideation more efficient, and it also makes ideation more rigorous. It stops you from daydreaming a harebrained idea and announcing: *I'm done!* It pushes you to keep iterating until you produce ideas that work.

This process of rational selection is convergent thinking. Convergent thinking pre-tests ideas via logical deduction, which uses known rules (of physics, psychology, and society) to compute whether an idea is tenuous or outright doomed.

Convergent thinking is the logical complement of divergent thinking (see below). It can also be employed, solo, to simplify existing processes (by eliminating their unnecessary features) or to refine existing products (by honing their core function).

2.3 Ideation: Its Major Random Processes

Randomness might not be a quality you associate with computation, but computers can be far more arbitrary than humans. If you ask a human to generate a list of random numbers, the human will go slowly and be biased toward certain digits. If you ask a computer, it will do so at electric speed with impartial haphazardness.[26]

Computers achieve this haphazardness by harvesting a random "seed" number (from a spontaneous source such as the computer's clock) and then running it through mathematical equations that amplify the initial instant of chance.[27] By applying logic to the arbitrary, computers are thus able to achieve superhuman randomness, allowing them to contribute to cryptography, cryptofinance – and also, creativity.

Randomness can contribute to creativity in different ways, but the three most influential are brainstorming, divergent thinking, and fixation disruption.

Brainstorming. The term *brainstorming* was coined in the 1940s by New York ad exec Alex Osborn.[28] As explained by Osborn, its literal origin is a military analogy: "*brainstorm* means using the brain to storm a creative problem – and do so in commando fashion, with each stormer attacking the same objective."[29]

---

[26] Wiggins 2006a, 2006b; Jing and Yang 2015; He et al. 2019; Mateja and Heinzl 2021; Lu et al. 2022; Lavrič and Škraba 2023; Franceschelli and Musolesi 2024.

[27] Deng and Lin 2000; Rahnamayan et al. 2008; Zenil 2011.   [28] Osborn 1963.

[29] Osborn 2008.

In the years since Osborn's coinage, brainstorming has taken on less martial connotations. It's now linked with mind-wandering, a process run by the brain's default mode network.[30] Mind-wandering is maximized when the brain's emotional anxieties and critical opinions are suspended. To boost brainstorming, experts therefore advise people to say whatever springs to mind, without judgment. The freer and more relaxed the proceedings, the more conducive to nonobvious ideas, nurturing novelty and hence creativity.

This process encourages our brain to randomly access our memory, stimulating a free association of ideas that can produce fresh analogies or disrupt fixation biases (see below).

Divergent Thinking. Take a concept. (Like *pineapple.*) Now connect it to a very different concept. (Like *bomb.*) What results from their combination? (A culinary explosion of sweet-and-sour? A grenade with a spikey shell?)[31]

The less that your two concepts have been previously associated, the more that they diverge.[32] Which is what gives this technique its name: *divergent* thinking.

Divergent thinking doesn't need to be limited to individual concepts. It can be used to associate disparate systems or patterns. What pops into your brain when you add a dinosaur to Greek mythology, or jellybeans to the Milky Way?

As these examples show, divergent thinking promotes analogical thinking. It pushes the brain to come up with maximally distant objects that the brain can then scan for patterns.

Fixation Disruption. Logical patterns can power creativity, but they can also hinder it. The better your brain gets at detecting a particular pattern, the less it pushes itself to see other patterns.

This is *fixation bias.*[33] It occurs when your brain gets stuck on certain designs, configurations, and models. It limits your imaginative reach and jams you in creative ruts.

To break free, hit your brain with random stuff. Indiscriminately grab books off library shelves. Travel to a faraway land or an obscure museum. Take the design you've drawn and turn it upside-down.

The more you engage in these haphazard activities, the more you'll jumble up your mental habits, spotting fresh opportunities.

---

[30] Abraham and Cramon 2009; Marron et al. 2018; Lopata et al. 2022.

[31] Boden 1996, 2004; Wiggins 2006a, 2006b; Franceschelli and Musolesi 2024.

[32] Hass 2017a, 2017b; Kenett 2018, 2019; Reiter-Palmon et al. 2019; Beaty et al. 2022.

[33] Wiley 1998; Frensch and Sternberg 2014; Youmans and Arciszewski 2014; Crilly 2015; Vasconcelos and Crilly 2016; Alipour et al. 2018; Storm et al. 2020.

There you have six ways to ideate: three via logic, three via randomness. This list is by no means exhaustive; computation can be leveraged in other ways to create new ideas. But this list is characteristic, which is to say, it accurately represents current creativity training. The rest of the training can be derived systematically from the principles and processes outlined above.

Although this list captures the big picture of modern creativity training, however, it fails to capture the fullness of human creativity, as we'll explore next.

3 What Current Creativity Training Misses

If you devoted yourself to ideation, rigorously excluding other processes from your mind, you'd get less effective at everyday problem-solving. Instead of increasing your natural creativity, you'd constrain it.

We'll discuss the scientific reasons for this in Section 4 (where we'll explore how creativity evolved in the brain) and in Section 10 (where we'll identify the mechanical limits of computation). But first, let's survey the current empirical evidence, from human and AI experiments, that ideation is missing something.

3.1 Empirical Evidence for the Limits of Ideation

Human Experiments. Ideation has produced underwhelming results in scientific trials. People trained in ideation perform better at ideation, which is to say, they improve at generating divergent concepts, ideal customers, and analogies.[34] But they don't show great improvement at solving problems or producing innovations.[35] Even long-term training in ideation does not yield significant results. Instead of steady improvement, it shows diminishing returns.[36]

To the extent that ideation does produce gains, moreover, they are in "minor" creativity: refinements or incremental improvements to existing ideas. This is perhaps to be expected in the case of design thinking and other logic-based techniques that emphasize optimization. But it also holds true in the case of randomization-based techniques. If you practice divergent thinking, you will get better at associating random concepts – but you will not become more likely to pioneer technology or revolutionize business.

AI Experiments. The limits of current creativity training could simply demonstrate the limits of humans. Humans, after all, aren't that logical – or that capable of randomness. Even when our brains are fully trained, our powers of

---

[34] Scott et al. 2004a, 2004b; Baer 2015.

[35] Brucks and Huang 2020; van Broekhoven et al. 2020; Ritter et al. 2020; Gonthier and Besançon 2022; Gu et al. 2022.

[36] Brucks and Huang 2020; Ritter et al. 2020.

design and brainstorming are bound to be imperfect. On this line of thinking, the reason that our species has succeeded is not because we're individually creative but because there are so many of us. The more people, the more random ideas, the more chance that one of those ideas is a breakthrough.[37] Training gains that seem insignificant at the level of individuals could yield huge payoffs at the level of populations.

We can test this hypothesis. We possess technology that can perform ideation at scale. That technology is: the computer.

The computer, as Guilford perceived many decades ago, is capable of both precision logic and massive randomness (see Section 2), allowing AI to accelerate ideation.[38] Brainstorming can be accomplished via random memory access; divergent thinking via mix-and-matching from sets; convergent thinking via pattern analysis of text and image libraries.[39] These operations have been automated by "generative" AI, which can run ideation at tremendous velocity. Large language models are capable of producing thousands of words a second, a rate of output that has astonished many observers into presuming that it is only a matter of time before AI fulfills Guilford's prediction and replaces human creatives.

That prediction is, however, contradicted by a simple empirical fact: LLMs do not improve by reading their own writing.[40] Instead, their performance degrades when they are trained on AI output.[41] This is in stark contrast to AI chess engines, which have increased their aptitude by playing each other until they have become capable of beating human grandmasters.[42]

The difference between AI chess engines and LLMs reveals that computers – despite the patterns that their logic circuits have found in previous human masterpieces – cannot determine the merits of new works. They cannot, that is, detect successful creations.[43] And this is fatal to their prospects of becoming innovators. The ability of computers to detect successful chess moves is why AIs can learn from playing themselves: When they execute a checkmate, they mark it for later use. But because computers cannot detect successful creations, LLMs cannot sift through their prodigious output for discoveries, self-educating.[44] Instead, the more words they produce, the more random bloat dilutes their effect.[45] LLMs improve only by reading human writers, or in other words, by copying our inventions. They are plagiarists, not creatives.

---

[37] Simonton 2015.   [38] Chen et al. 2019.   [39] Hubert et al. 2024; Minai et al. 2021.

[40] Wong 2024.

[41] Shumailov et al. 2023; Shumailov et al., 2024; Dohmatob, Feng, Yang et al. 2024; Dohmatob, Feng, and Kempe 2024.

[42] Hassabis 2017; Risi and Preuss 2020; Gaessler and Piezunka 2023.   [43] Wang et al. 2019.

[44] For example, West et al. 2023.   [45] Shumailov et al. 2023.

The inability to identify and build on creative successes has prevented AI from generating breakthrough art, science, technology, or business.[46] Sometimes, AI brainstorms have inspired artists and entrepreneurs. And sometimes, AI has brute-forced solutions to problems defined by scientists and engineers. But without the added ingredient of human intelligence, AI creativity has proved of limited utility.

AI's creative deficit has been rationalized in a variety of ways: *AI needs improved software. Or, better data. Or, consciousness.* But AI's failure to replicate human creativity doesn't result from a shortcoming of current computers. It results from a shortcoming of the theory that creativity is computational.

3.2 How We Know That Creativity Is More than Computational

Here are some human creatives: Leonardo DaVinci, William Shakespeare, Vincent van Gogh, Marie Curie, Albert Einstein, Frida Kahlo, Grace Hopper, Steve Jobs.

These creatives weren't random. They were disciplined and intentional. They had a method for generating their insights and inventions. Yet that method wasn't logic. Logic produces universality, while that method nurtured individual styles of inquiry and production. Van Gogh's use of color was highly unconventional. Einstein's theories contradicted the rational deductions of eminent physicists. Steve Jobs was credited with a "reality-distortion" field.[47]

But how is it possible for a method to be nonlogical? And what could that nonlogic be?

We can glimpse the answer in analogical, design, and divergent thinking. When these processes run on human brains, they often drift beyond computation, getting "ghost help" from mental activities that can't be reduced to symbolic logic's AND/OR/NOT operations:

- *Ghost Help One.* When humans deploy analogical thinking, they don't stick to analogies of structure; they instead imagine analogies of function.[48] That is, rather than strictly performing pattern recognition, humans also perform *process* recognition. They go beyond computing configurations, shapes, and designs to compare sequences of action.
- *Ghost Help Two.* Design thinking begins with empathy. Granted, it is not full, human empathy. Full, human empathy focuses on what is distinct about persons, exploring the uniqueness of individual minds.[49] Design empathy

---

[46] As Margaret Boden has noted, computational creativity is "exploratory" rather than "transformational." For more, see Boden 1996, 2004; Wiggins 2006a, 2006b; 2019; Eppe et al. 2018; Carnovalini and Rodà 2020.

[47] Fletcher 2025.

[48] For example, Alan Turing's discussion of "analogies of function" as a basis for how humans can engineer computers. In Turing 1950.

[49] Grant and Berry 2011; Glăveanu 2015; Keenan-Lechel et al. 2019; Glăveanu 2020.

instead involves a generalized abstraction: the ideal user.[50] Yet even that abstract empathy exceeds AI. No algorithm can empathize with a human user, because the wants and needs of that user are informed by emotion and other nonlogical operations.

• *Ghost Help Three.* Divergent thinking is rigorously defined in logic as the measure of divergence between an idea's components.[51] But in school and business brainstorming sessions, it's typically used to connote a diversity of human perspectives, and those perspectives are (as in *Ghost Help Two*) informed by emotion and other nonlogical operations.[52]

This ghost help can't be magic or ineffable. The human brain is a biological machine. All its operations are physical. So, what physical operation could run sequences of action, latch onto unique human motivations, and contain multiple people's perspectives?

The answer is: narrative. Narrative is the nonlogical, nonrandom, physical operation that enables the brain to perform process recognition, empathy, and perspective-shifting. To understand how narrative does this, let's delve into the biology of where narrative came from – and what it evolved to do.

4 Narrative's Role in Creativity

The human brain is a computer – and also more.

That more can be felt every time your brain departs from what *is* to speculate on what *could happen*. Such speculation isn't mathematical approximation, statistical probability, or fuzzy logic. Those are all potential states of being, or in other words, *could be*. And *could be* is different from *could happen*. *Could happen* is action, not being. Instead of probable truths, now and forever, it's possible causes and effects, past and future. It's hypothesized mechanisms that cannot be proven. It's posited innovations that aren't guaranteed.

The psychological term for this brain action is *imagination*. Imagination is what Guilford attempted to distill to ideation. Partly, he did so because imagination seemed too numinous a thing to be taught rigorously in classrooms. But he also did so because imagination had a reputation of devolving into idle guessing and irrational bias, going beyond *could happen* into *could never happen*, duping minds into self-delusion and stretching facts into flat-out fiction.

Imagination's tendency to veer into the impossible is why logic originated in the first place. It was concern over the dangers of literary fantasy that prompted the

---

[50] Brown and Katz 2011; Kolko 2014; Brown 2019; Koskinen 2023.

[51] Hass 2017b; Kenett et al. 2017; Kenett 2018, 2019; Reiter-Palmon et al. 2019; Orwig et al. 2021; Beaty et al. 2022.

[52] Kalargiros and Manning 2015; Paulus and Kenworthy 2019.

fourth-century BCE Athenian philosopher Plato to call for societies that stuck entirely to the laws of reason. In answer to that call, Plato's student Aristotle distilled logic to the three rules of AND/OR/NOT that drove the syllogisms of medieval theology and continue to drive computer AI today (see Section 2).

But while imagination has a long history of making philosophers nervous, it has an even longer history of helping the rest of us thrive, as we can see by turning back to our brain's origins and discovering what *could happen* evolved to do.

4.1 The Origins of *Could Happen*

Our brain is composed of billions of neurons. Yet in the beginning, it was just a single neuron.[53] That neuron evolved more than 525 million years ago, during the Cambrian Period.[54] Before then, animals were mostly floaters and bobbers. They survived not by pursuing food but by encountering it.

The archaic neuron changed this, imbuing life with intention.[55] The intention came from two different functions, the first of which was vision. Vision worked by inducting data. That data took the form of light, which either was there – or wasn't.[56] The earliest vision neurons thus operated in binary ON/OFF. They signaled (i.e., represented) the presence or absence of things to eat.[57]

Binary, induction, and symbolic representation are all logic functions. And as vision got more advanced, these logic functions developed.[58] Vision neurons formed circuits that ran basic AND/OR/NOT operations. Those circuits eventually developed into the animal visual cortex, which could synthesize vast amounts of inducted data into three-dimensional, real-time representations of the outside environment.[59]

The visual cortex was a symbolic logic processor. Which is to say: It was a computer. Like a modern AI, it used logic to detect spatial patterns. And from those patterns, it identified potential prey and adversaries.

Over long millennia, the neurons that performed these logical tasks propagated to other regions of what became the human neocortex. Those regions became good at mathematics, pattern recognition (along with its related functions, generalization, abstraction, and design), and representational language (such as nouns, adjectives, and linking verbs).[60] They were able to compute true, false, and *could be.*

---

[53] Moroz and Romanova 2022.

[54] Budd and Jackson 2016; Liebeskind et al. 2016, 2017; Kristan 2016; Ortega-Hernández et al. 2019.

[55] Moroz and Kohn 2016; Williams 2016; Schwab 2018.   [56] Asteriti et al. 2015.

[57] Rosa and Krubitzer 1999; Kaas 2020.

[58] Houdé and Tzourio-Mazoyer 2003; Knauff 2007; Monti and Osherson 2012; Vinod et al. 2017.

[59] Ma et al. 2012.   [60] Houdé and Tzourio-Mazoyer 2003.

These processes were useful. Very, very useful. But they were not enough to enable our ancestors to survive the primordial struggle for life. That survival also required the archaic neuron's second function: action.[61]

Action does not require a neuron. Ancient animals evolved flagellums, water jets, and muscles that operated autonomously, without a nervous system. But these sources of motion had limited capacity for learning, direction, and innovation, a capacity massively enlarged by the development of neurons that could initiate, sequence, and record new actions.[62]

Actions were different from data. Data was timeless mathematical coordinates. Actions were causes and effects, which occurred in pasts and futures outside logic's eternal present.[63]

While vision-processing benefited hunters by helping them pursue food, action-processing benefited the hunted by helping them initiate evasive maneuvers. Those maneuvers were most effective not when they were random but when they anticipated the hunter's intent and surprised it. Thus was born innovation, the power that now drives the dynamic fluidity of the legs of athletes, the fingers of musicians, and the faces of comic actors.

Over time, in the same way that visual neurons developed more advanced structures and capabilities, so did action neurons. They networked to form brain regions that ran *could happen*, plotting future behaviors and speculating on the causes of past occurrences. Those brain operations were not symbolic logic.[64] They were narrative cognition. Or, more colloquially, storythinking.[65]

Storythinking is thinking in causes, not correlations, in mechanisms, not patterns. Instead of analyzing life into numbers, equations, relations, and labels,

---

[61] O'Regan and Noë 2001; Monk and Paulin 2014; Fletcher 2023.

[62] Tsodyks et al. 1999; Keijzer et al. 2013; Fu et al. 2019.   [63] See Section 10.1.

[64] Causation was assumed to be logical by medieval Scholastic philosophers, but this assumption was challenged during the eighteenth-century Enlightenment by David Hume. Hume defined causality as a propensity of the human mind, offering first an associationist account and later a counterfactual account for the attribution of causality (Hume 1986; Hume and Steinberg 1993). Then, in the early twentieth century, Bertrand Russell, the logician who helped found modern analytic and mathematical philosophy, declared causation non-existent because it could not be proven logically (Russell 1912). Over the past hundred years, the claims of Hume and Russell have led modern philosophers to treat causality empirically and descriptively, rather than logically (Davidson 1963, 1967; Mackie 1980; Goodman 1983; Dupré 1993; Salmon 1998; Strawson 2014; Mercier and Sperber 2017). One modern philosophical approach is to understand causality via interventions and counterfactuals; this empirical turn underlies statistical and probabilistic definitions of causation (Lewis 1973; Lewis 1979; Woodward 2005; Pearl 2009b). A second approach is to stress the materiality of causal powers as something beyond logical models yet irreducibly real (Harré and Madden 1975; Cartwright 2002, 2016; Bhaskar 2020). A third approach is to emphasize that causality's psychological dimension reflects its status as a mode of human cognition rather than an objective set of logical operations (Sloman and Sloman 2009; Michotte 2017; Campbell 2020).

[65] Fletcher 2023.

it uses narrative tools such as character, plot, storyworld, and narrator, each of which evolved for a biological function.

- *Character.* This is a tool for processing the psychological and physical mechanics of living organisms. It evolved because those organisms (including the organisms of one's own species) are life's primary threats and opportunities.
- *Plot.* This is a tool for combining, sequencing, and interacting mechanisms, making it possible to hypothesize the causes of unexpected events and the effects of unprecedented plans. It evolved to power active learning and behavioral innovation.
- *Storyworld.* This is a tool for speculating on what is possible in any given environment. It evolved because biological environments are imbued with dynamic instability, necessitating the imagination of new paths to food and reproduction.
- *Narrator.* This is a tool for integrating the brain's personal *why* (i.e., its own life motive) with its environment. It evolved to help the brain develop long-term strategies that promote intentional conduct in volatile situations.

Storythinking, like logic, propagated across the human cortex. It now powers brain regions that are good at planning, process recognition, and narrative language (e.g., action verbs). These regions allow us to probe *how* and *why*. They make us creative strategists and canny leaders. They supplement the eternal truth of logic with the *could happen* of imagination.

That's the story of how two kinds of intelligence, logic and narrative, came to function side-by-side in our heads. Until in our own day, they were broken apart.

4.2 How Logic Displaced Narrative Intelligence in Modern Education

Creativity training isn't the only twenty-first-century curriculum based on logic. Logic has become the foundation of most academic instruction, from elementary school through executive MBA. Narrative is rarely trained, even in fields such as literature and communication. Those fields instead prioritize critical thinking, interpretation, and other logic-based skills. When they do teach stories, they teach it as themes, archetypes, representations, plot structures, and other logical abstractions.

Modern education got this way for many reasons, but the main three are: the skew of consciousness, the bias of logic, and the emphasis on standardized assessments.

The Skew of Consciousness. Our brain possesses self-awareness, which tricks us into thinking that we're aware of our self. But in fact, we're aware of only a small fraction of the goings-on that constitute our biology. Our mind can't perceive the workings of our gut or heart. It doesn't even know the majority of what's occurring inside our brain.[66]

What our mind does know, moreover, is dominated by vision.[67] Vision, for most of us, is the focus of our consciousness. We're heavily aware of the illuminated environment around, and when darkness makes that environment unseeable, we close our eyes and go to sleep, slipping into nonconsciousness.

Vision's hefty role in consciousness, and consciousness' equally hefty role in self-awareness, can lead our mind into believing that thinking is fundamentally analogous to seeing.[68] And seeing is a product of symbolic logic (Section 4.1). It's generated by the part of our cortex that operates like a computer. The more that we believe that thought is based in visual processes such as pattern-finding and data calculation, the more that we equate intelligence with computation,[69] neglecting (and even denying) the alternative neural operations of narrative.

This is the error made by many philosophers of mind, back through the Enlightenment to Plato. And it's the same mistake that many design thinkers, AI engineers, and cognitive scientists are making now.

The Bias of Logic. Logic styles itself as a tool for eliminating bias. Yet there's one bias that logic cannot see, let alone eradicate: its bias toward itself. Its bias, that is, toward logic.[70]

When logic encounters nonlogical forms of intelligence such as scientific hypothesis, commonsense inference, and causal speculation, it equates them with statistics, symbolic math, and Bayesian networks.[71] It reduces human neurons, despite their enormous physical variety and anatomical complexity, to simple ON/OFF switches, treating the brain as no more than a sense-making apparatus that operates algorithmically. To suppose otherwise, it thinks, is to wander into magic, superstition, and pseudoscience.

But narrative is not magic. It is a set of physical mechanisms that complement logic by performing tasks that logic cannot. Logic is useful in stable, transparent

---

[66] Brogaard 2011.   [67] Pins and Ffytche 2003; Kupers et al. 2011.

[68] This analogy is the basis of the term *Enlightenment*, which refers to an intellectual movement (historically situated in seventeenth and eighteenth-century Europe, but with long roots and diffuse branches) that identifies itself with logic.

[69] Fukushima 1988; Zhang et al. 2020.

[70] Shenefelt and White 2013; Mercier and Sperber 2017.

[71] For more on the relationship between causal insight, empiricism, and probabilistic and interventionist causal models, see Pearl 1993, 2009b; Gopnik and Schulz 2007; Gopnik et al. 2004; Schölkopf et al. 2021; Cartwright 1979, 2007; Chou et al. 2022; Kosoy et al. 2022.

environments where enduring truths can be computed. Narrative is useful in volatile, murky environments where original actions must be ventured. Logic is big data. Narrative is low (even no) information. Logic is spatial patterns. Narrative is mechanical processes. Logic is timeless. Narrative is change. Logic abstracts and generalizes. Narrative leverages the specific and individual. Logic seeks synthesis. Narrative is fed by conflict.

Narrative values difference, allowing it to respect logic as an equal partner. Logic, however, values identities, which is to say, unities. So, it seeks to incorporate narrative into a single system of logical processes. Within that system, narrative is used not for thinking but for communicating, or in other words, for conveying ideas that logic has validated. This is why modern schools and businesses associate narrative with marketing and logic with innovation, denying story a fundamental role in creative problem-solving and invention.

Standardized Assessments. Assessment is crucial for learning. Biologically, assessment originates in self-appraisal, which by gauging whether our actions advance our personal goals, enables us to grow intentionally. Socially, assessment extends to mentoring and teaching, through which we help others develop their distinctive skills and abilities.

Free societies have historically tolerated wide latitude in assessment, leaving it largely to the discretion of individual learning communities. But in the twentieth century, the rise of industrial democracy prompted a shift toward standardized assessments.[72] Such assessments could be graded algorithmically, making them more efficient to administer. And because they had objectively right and wrong answers, they were perceived as more fair.[73] They allowed more students to be appraised with less cultural bias and teacherly caprice, powering the spread of meritocracy.

Standardized tests are now staples of K-12 education, where they drive state funding, teacher promotion, and student placement.[74] Standardized metric evaluations are also core to most large corporations, where they direct hiring, performance reviews, and salary. And as they have themselves been assessed and improved, they have become more objective and more efficient. Yet the results have not been unambiguously positive.[75]

In business, standardized assessments have hampered imagination, contradicted commonsense, and perpetuated prejudice. In schools, standardized assessments have motivated "teaching to the test," and because they test logical operations such as math and memorization, they have channeled instruction

---

[72] Garrison 2009; Rury 2023; Lemann 2024. [73] Harris et al. 2011; Beach 2021; Rury 2023.
[74] Harris et al. 2011; Kempf 2016; Beach 2021; Rury 2023.
[75] Harris et al. 2011; Kempf 2016; Koretz 2017; Muller 2019; Gottlieb 2020.

away from poems, plays, novels, and other narrative works. For millennia, across cultures, those works were used to nurture imagination, emotional development, and general wisdom. Yet now, they are quantified via essay rubrics and multiple-choice exams that reduce books to snippets, writing to formulas, and reading to keyword hunting.

4.3 Reviving Narrative

Even though logic pervades our twenty-first-century schools and workplaces, narrative is still there. It's embedded in our neuroanatomy. It's a root process of our brain's default mode network.[76] It springs into action every time we make a plan for *how* – or ask *why* things happen.

And although modern schools and workplaces don't have a curriculum for strengthening narrative intelligence, that curriculum can be found in the world's libraries and museums, as we will explore next section.

5 Narrative Creativity Training, the Prehistory

Narrative is a product of creativity. That's the standard view taught at school today. But narrative can also be a *source* of creativity. It can be an engine of new actions, new plans, new solutions to problems.

Narrative, in other words, can be more than storytelling. It can be story*thinking*.[77]

5.1 The Scholarly Discovery of Storythinking

The first modern scholars to study narrative's creative powers were twentieth-century education researchers who noticed young children imagining themselves as doctors, parents, soldiers, homemakers, and leaders. While playing those roles, the children used stories to solve hypothetical problems – and to invent medicines, tools, and plans.[78]

This childhood method of narrative creativity was promoted in the 1990s by Anna Craft. Born in 1961 in Lancashire, England, Craft received her B.A. in Social and Political Science from Cambridge University, and then obtained a Master's in Education. After teaching briefly in a London primary school, she worked as a professor at Open University, Harvard University, and Exeter University. She established the Centre for Creativity Research in Education and published *Creativity Across the Primary Curriculum* (2000) and *Creativity and Early Years Education* (2002). Until in 2014, at the age of fifty-two, she died of cancer.

---

[76] Abraham 2016, 2018; Carroll 2020.   [77] Fletcher 2023.
[78] Craft 2004, 2015; Vygotsky 2004; Cremin et al. 2013; Chappell, Cremin, and Jeffrey 2015; Russ and Zyga 2016; Cremin 2017; Chylińska and Gut 2020; Lee and Russ 2021.

Craft's research focused on *possibility thinking*, a narrative process based on *what-if* (i.e., counterfactual) thinking.[79] It's used by children to roleplay, creatively experiment, and generate alternate realities. To nurture possibility thinking, Craft and her team developed exercises that emphasized theatrical improvisation and story sharing, inviting students to roam through imaginative worlds that freed them from adult judgments, standardized tests, and RIGHT/WRONG answers.

These exercises weren't, as Craft was quick to observe, her invention. They'd been devised by children in prehistoric ages. Craft's contribution was to circulate, refine, and validate them. And even that contribution, richly original though it was, had not originated with her. It had begun thousands of years earlier in archaic theater and literature.

5.2 The Origins of Story Science

The first known theaters were erected in ancient Greece, more than 2500 years ago. But it's likely that informal stages and performances occurred long before, at primeval gatherings and campfires.

Literature's origins are likewise archaic – and murky. The world's first known author is Enheduanna, a Sumerian poet-priest who styled herself an "inventor" of written literature.[80] But we can guess that oral literature is older still, its roots extending before the origin of our species.[81]

Why did theater and literature evolve? The answers long favored by scholars are: (1) entertainment and (2) instruction. In support of (1), stage performances can be fun, and in support of (2), fables can be appended with Aesopian morals or interpreted as allegories. Yet even so, these scholarly answers miss the obvious. If you ask children why they enjoy puppet shows and storybooks, they will tell you: *Because I like to use my imagination.*

That use of imagination can be more than idle play. It can nurture creativity. Children's literature – from classic nursery rhymes like *Hey Diddle Diddle* to modern fare like *Winnie-the-Pooh* – is filled with narrative techniques for activating the default mode network,[82] stimulating the brain to invent new characters, plots, and storyworlds.

Literature's creative powers stay with us long after childhood. Those powers have been felt by every adult who has viewed a movie and tried to guess its ending; or consumed a sci-fi story and speculated on living in the future; or watched a detective show and tried to solve the mystery; or read a memoir and imagined acting like the author. In all these cases, literature has encouraged

---

[79] Craft et al. 2013; Cremin et al. 2013; Craft 2015; Craft and Chappell 2016.
[80] Fletcher 2021b, Preface.   [81] Fletcher 2021b, Preface.   [82] Fletcher 2021b, chapter 18.

storythinking. It has prompted the brain to roleplay, hypothesize on narrative outcomes, explore imaginary worlds, or devise original actions.

By motivating storythinking, literature can help us become authors of our own films and novels. And it can go beyond enriching our literary skills; it can also develop our capacities at politics, science, engineering, business, and warfare. The political and technological inventions of Niccolò Machiavelli and Leonardo DaVinci were kindled by their studies of ancient comedy and mythology. Albert Einstein, Mary Shelley, Marie Curie, and Carl von Clausewitz were inspired by the Romantic revival of Shakespeare, while Vincent van Gogh, Dr. William Osler, Nikola Tesla, Maya Angelou, and Steve Jobs credited their imaginative achievements directly to Shakespeare himself.[83]

How did narrative generate the practical breakthroughs of innovators like these? Next section, we'll extend Anna Craft's research to see.

6 Narrative Creativity Training, a New Theory

When we read a story, we don't just process what's in front of our eyes. We also imagine what's to come.[84]

That imagining is obvious when we read serial fiction. Serial fiction is broken into episodes, each of which ends with a cliffhanger that provokes the question: *What will happen next?* To answer that question, our mind ventures possibilities, glimpsing events beyond the page.

This mental process isn't limited to serial fiction. It occurs more subtly with every story. The moment we start reading, our brain begins to speculate on the story's future. That speculation is why we flip faster through books (and even skip right to the end), hungry to test our guesses. It's why we feel suspense when we're immersed in romances and thrillers, as we foresee our heroes marrying the wrong person (*horror!*) or outwitting their adversaries (*hurrah!*). And it's why we continue novels and movies past their endings, imaginatively roleplaying characters and mind-wandering through storyworlds long after we're done reading.

How does our brain do this? How does it intuit where the plot might go? How does it create what the author has not written?

6.1 What Happens in Our Brain When We Read (or Watch) Stories

Every action has a cause. That cause is an earlier action. Sometimes the earlier action is easy to spot. But often, it's hidden, partly or fully. We know it only through its effect.

---

[83] Fletcher 2025.
[84] Brooks 1992; Sternberg 1992, 2003; Carroll 2001; Herman 2009, 2017; Kukkonen 2020.

This is why we're often forced to guess about why things happen. When someone acts shockingly, we cannot know for certain what they were thinking, only speculate about their motives. The same goes for when life delivers us a plot-twist: We must guess about unseen rules of society, politics, economics, or physics.

Such guessing can be fruitful. But often, it's not. Often, our brain leaps to a vague, general explanation: *People are selfish . . . Life is unpredictable.* These explanations allow our brain to move on and focus on other problems. Yet they also prevent our brain from learning. They keep us from gaining deeper clarity about how the world works. They cost us the opportunity to discover new psychological and physical mechanisms that we could use to better grasp – and influence – what happens next.

Literature restores that opportunity by entering us into the motives of characters and by exposing the mechanics of storyworlds. This exposition is particularly evident in comedies of manners, fantasy novels, sci-fi movies, and other stories where characters (or the narrator) explain the rules of dating, magic systems, and new technologies. But exposition can also occur less explicitly. Any time a story focuses on a particular event sequence, simplifying the world's hurly-burly to a tidy narrative, it's telling our brain: *This cause produced that effect. It's why and how that action occurred.*

By providing our brain with access to causes, stories allow our brain to do more than understand what has happened. They allow our brain to speculate on what *will* happen. Once we know the nuts and bolts of a character's psychology, we can race ahead of the narrative to hypothesize how the character might react. Once we grasp a storyworld's rules of action, we can anticipate its potential plot-twists.

Such storythinking isn't always fully conscious.[85] It whirs along in deep brain regions, registering in our sentient mind as flickering intuitions. But you can confirm its existence by reading badly executed fiction. Whenever a narrative's action seems implausible, that's your brain thinking: *That sequence of events violates the mechanics of this storyworld.* Same goes for whenever you frown at a character's uncharacteristic behavior: *They would never do that!*

You wouldn't have those reactions if reading was a passive computational process of inputting printed words into your brain. You have those reactions because your brain is actively storythinking, leaping from known causes to likely effects.[86] The specific learning acquired via this imaginative leaping isn't always useful: Mastering the mechanics of a fantasy world may not help us

---

[85] Abraham 2016, 2018; Zhu et al. 2017; Fabry and Kukkonen 2019; Carroll 2020; Russ 2020.

[86] Bridgeman 2005; Radvansky and Zacks 2014; Simony et al. 2016; Song et al. 2021.

navigate our daily lives. Yet the general action of using literature to prompt storythinking can be very useful indeed. It allows us to practice narrative conjecture in settings that are simpler and more transparent than real life. It helps us exercise the mental muscles that our brain uses to adapt to new social and physical environments. And it attunes us to the deeper method of narrative creativity.

6.2 The Method of Narrative Creativity: From *Why* to *What if*

Before your brain can imagine the end of a story, it has to grasp the beginning. Which is to say: The first step in creative thinking is causal thinking. It's determining – or, more commonly, speculating – *why* previous things happened the way that they did.[87] It's hypothesizing hidden mechanisms of psychology, society, and physics.

Once your brain has a theory about those mechanisms, it can incorporate the theory into a narrative thought experiment: It can change a fact about the present, insert that fact into its theorized mechanism, and imagine what happens next. It can, that is, engage in counterfactual (aka *what-if*) thinking, conjecturing the effects of speculative causes.

Biologically, this process evolved to allow our brain to adapt to shifting environments. The process begins when our brain is surprised by an event. That event's unexpectedness reveals the insufficiency of our existing narrative about the world, prompting our brain to realize that there must be more to the story of life. Perhaps the more is a new threat; perhaps it's a new opportunity. Either way, the unexpected event came from a previously unseen source – and the better that we can grasp the source, the more that we can avoid or exploit it in the future.

Put in narrative terms: When we're surprised by an event, our brain realizes that we've arrived in the *middle* of an unknown story.[88] To learn the rest of the story, we must imaginatively rewind time to hypothesize the story's *beginning*, conjecturing the event's origins. Then, to test our hypothesis, we must anticipate the story's *end*, predicting what happens next. Even though we think of stories as running from beginning to middle to end, storythinking thus evolved in our brain to run: *middle → beginning → end*.

When running this process, it's more efficient to explain the unexpected in terms of the known, or in other words, to trace new events to familiar causes. But that efficiency limits our effectiveness in dynamic environments, so our

---

[87] Buchsbaum et al. 2012; Gopnik and Walker 2013; Byrne 2016; Roese and Epstude 2017; Parikh et al. 2018.

[88] Roese 1997; Byrne 2002; Epstude and Roese 2011; Van Hoeck 2015.

brain has evolved the capacity to imagine new mechanisms that we can practically test – the capacity, in other words, to perform causal invention and counterfactual experiment.[89] The former is the driver of science; the latter of cultural and technological innovation.

Causal invention and counterfactual experiment are engines of creative thinking. When our brain uses possible causes to generate possible effects, it breaks free from what *is* to generate what *could happen* (see Section 4). Such breaking free is how authors create original stories. And it's also how engineers create original technologies, how scientists create original hypotheses, how entrepreneurs create original goods and services, how doctors create original medicines and therapies, and how leaders create original laws and strategies. All employ the same causal–counterfactual method: converting a conjectured mechanism of action into a possible plot, or in other words, a future plan.

The key to consistent and sustainable gains in narrative creativity is to practice this method, which, to cliffhanger you, is what we'll do in the next section.

7 Narrative Creativity Training, Basic Practices

Causal and counterfactual thinking are innate to our brain.[90] But both can be made more rigorous with practice.[91] That practice decreases magical thinking and boosts innovation.

Causal thinking gets more rigorous when we focus on unique causes, each with its own distinct mechanical operations and effects.[92] Counterfactual thinking gets more rigorous when we focus on specific, step-by-step results of manipulating a single cause.

All of which adds up to: We increase our real-world creativity (1) by *diversifying* causal thinking and (2) by *sharpening* counterfactual thinking. The first supplies more prompts for our imagination; the second, more precise plans for us to try.

7.1 Diversifying Causal Thinking

We diversify our causal thinking every time we add a new cause to our mental catalogue. The more specific the cause – that is, the more clearly that it can be mechanically distinguished from other causes – the more diversity it adds.

---

[89] Magnani 2009; Pearl 2009b; Lombrozo 2012; Johnson-Laird and Khemlani 2017; Goddu and Gopnik 2024.
[90] Hume 1986, 1993; Gopnik and Schulz 2007; Sloman and Sloman 2009; Campbell 2020.
[91] Cheng and Buehner 2012; Waismeyer and Meltzoff 2017; Lagnado and Sloman 2019; Goddu and Gopnik 2020; Fletcher and Benveniste 2022; Fletcher et al. 2023.
[92] Sloman and Lagnado 2015; Lagnado and Sloman 2019.

We can add diversity by imagining new causes from scratch, as when we invent a tool. But more commonly, we add diversity via the discovery of causal mechanisms. That discovery is driven by explanation-seeking, which occurs when we hypothesize from an observed effect to an unseen causal mechanism, asking: *Why* did that happen – and *how?*[93]

Explanation-seeking is natural for children. It's the reason they're always asking *why?* And it's how they discover social and physical rules that help them navigate and influence the world.[94] As we age into adulthood, however, we focus more on fact-seeking. In fact-seeking, we ask: *What happened, when did it happen, and where?* We search for new data, not new mechanisms.

We make this transition toward fact-seeking because our adult brain has settled on a mental model of the world. When we observe an event, we don't pause, as a child would do, in wonder.[95] Instead we say: *I know why that happened.* Rather than seeing an opportunity to learn, we see a chance to display mastery. Displaying mastery is efficient, allowing us to rapidly process information and execute actions. And it works well, as long as the environment is stable. Mastery breaks down, however, in times of volatility. Volatility brings new threats and opportunities, or in other words, new causes of failure and success. To grasp those causes and leverage them, our brain needs to shift back to its childhood way of seeking new explanations. But often, our brain has been so conditioned to trust its current explanations that it cannot make the shift. Instead, it rationalizes unprecedented events as consequences of familiar factors.

This tendency is especially pronounced when our brain subscribes to an ideology. Ideology is a product of logic, which traces events to timeless principles such as justice, evil, and capital. Ideology convinces us that we already have the explanation for unusual occurrences, prompting us to make confident judgments that forestall us from imagining fresh *whys* and *hows*. By doing so, ideology hampers adaptation and innovation. We're not able to develop new courses of action when our brain is stuck thinking in the same old causal mechanisms.

We can unstick our brain via a simple method: focusing on anomalies. Anomalies are events that don't conform to our mental rules of society and physics, so they stir curiosity, prompting explanation-seeking.[96] Anomalies do

---

[93] Sloman 2009; Cheng and Buehner 2012; Gopnik et al. 2013; Walker and Lombrozo 2017; Liquin and Lombrozo 2020a; Liquin and Lombrozo 2020b; Kosoy et al. 2022; Goddu and Gopnik 2024.

[94] Callanan and Oakes 1992; Alvarez and Booth 2015; Legare et al. 2017; Basch and Wang 2024.

[95] Lucas et al. 2014; Samland 2016; Liquin and Gopnik 2022.

[96] Kahneman and Miller 1986; Kahneman 1995; Roese 1997; Roese and Olson 1997; Mandel 2003.

that prompting naturally, but in our modern world, their biological force has been muted by logic. To regain the benefit of anomalies, we must therefore consciously reverse how logic conditions our brain to treat them.

Logic conditions our brain to treat anomalies as random variance, blips to be regressed to the mean, noise that distracts from a consistent signal. Logic does this because it reduces life to mathematical models. Mathematical models can be remarkably good at predicting weather systems, political contests, and even military conflicts, yet they are never completely accurate. The mathematical rationalization for that remarkably good but not perfect accuracy is: *Logic deals in probabilities, percentages, and other approximations.* The rationalization is not wrong, yet it is misleading, because it obscures the mechanical reasons for model performance. Mechanically, a model is accurate insofar as it mathematically represents the material causes that drive events. When a model is good but not perfect, it is thus accounting for some but not all the causes.

Those unmodeled causes can't be discovered if anomalies are dismissed as the inherent noise of statistical probabilities. And they also can't be derived from pattern-finding, regression analysis, or other logical explorations of anomalous datapoints. Such explorations are correlational, so they lead to overfitting. In overfitting, a model gets better at rationalizing existing data but worse at predicting future events.[97] Overfitting is an endemic issue for AI, and it also occurs persistently in statistical analyses of biological systems, because of their enormous mechanical variety.[98]

To excavate that variety, we need to exit logic and return to treating anomalies as our brain naturally does: as prompts for explanation-seeking, or in other words, as prompts for hypothesizing unmodeled causal mechanisms. Adults are more effective than children at such hypothesizing, but children are more likely to attempt it, because children are more likely to value anomalies.[99] Adults can, however, increase the number of anomalies they value. They simply have to suspend their learned habits of logical efficiency – categorizing, identifying, labeling – and attend to cherishing the differences between individuals.

That cherishing is why children treat all items as special. A six-month-old will hesitate, scowl, and even cry if her toy is replaced with a toy that looks the same to adult eyes. In her infant mind, no two toys can be identical, because every toy is unique. This belief in the individuality of objects can seem irrational, but it is physically accurate. The experienced artisan knows: Each tool has its own distinct properties. That hammer does not strike like this one,

---

[97] Domingos 2000; Hawkins 2004; Bilbao and Bilbao 2017; Ying 2019.

[98] Subramanian and Simon 2013; Kosoy et al. 2022.

[99] Glăveanu 2011; Cassotti et al. 2016; Walker et al. 2016; Bergey et al. 2020; Goddu et al. 2020; Goddu et al. 2021; Gualtieri and Finn 2022.

nor does this saw cut like that one. Outside the idealized realm of mathematics, all objects are individual causes. Physics equations are no more than helpful approximations.

What's true of physical objects also holds for human psychologies. Those psychologies are birthed via biological processes – such as sexual reproduction and genetic recombination – that promote functional diversity, a diversity grown further through life experiences. Thus it is that every brain has its own particular motives, emotions, and intents – its own character.

To realize this is to open ourselves to genuine empathy, as distinct from design thinking's logical use of "empathy" to homogenize humanity into idealized users.[100] And to realize this is also to open ourselves to modern science. Modern science is often mischaracterized as the belief that all physical events (from planetary rotations to human heartbeats) are reducible to algorithmic formulas. But that belief existed in the Middle Ages. What changed in the Renaissance was the discovery that astral bodies weren't all made of the same heavenly substance, quintessence.[101] Different stars and planets had different physical natures. The skies were full of diversity – and singularity. The future of science lay not in the deductive application of known rules but in the discovery of exceptions that drove the development of new hypotheses. To understand the world, scientists needed more than math and logic; they needed conjecture and experiment.

To help you transition into this imaginative approach to life, Sections 8 and 9 will provide exercises for diversifying causal thinking. But the key to the transition is wanting to make it.[102] The more that you recognize the practical value of treating other people, social happenings, and biological events as unique occurrences, the more that you can discover new causes.

7.2 Sharpening Counterfactual Thinking

It's easy to imagine alternate worlds. Worlds in which we're superheroes. Worlds in which everyone is charmed by our wit and wisdom. Worlds in which we visualize success – and it happens. But that kind of imagining isn't fruitful creativity. It's magical thinking.

Magical thinking is common in children, which is why adults often equate imagination with wishful dreams. Yet children don't fall into fantasy because there's a necessary link between creativity and magical thinking. Children are simply less experienced in the micro-mechanics of nature and society, so they

---

[100] Brown and Katz 2011; Kolko 2014; Koskinen 2023.   [101] Galilei 1953, pp. 106, 474.
[102] Plucker and Dow 2017.

don't perceive all the distinct physical steps needed to achieve the outcomes they envision.

Children can, however, learn those steps. And they *do* learn, every day. Which is why billions of children succeed in their journey to navigate the world effectively enough to fulfill their basic needs – and to satisfy at least some of their larger aspirations.

Children succeed in this journey because of a gradual honing of counterfactual thinking.[103] Counterfactual thinking is engaged naturally by our brain as a consequence of failure.[104] Every time we experience a setback or disappointment, our brain plays back the sequence of events and thinks: *What if I did something different?*[105]

What if isn't always constructive. It can lead to unproductive regret, shame, or dissociation. But its benefits can be maximized if we

1. Anatomize *why* and *how* the failure occurred. What, exactly, went sideways? What were the specific steps – and the particular physical, social, or psychological mechanisms – that played out? Can we rewind the failure in our mind and replay it, sharpening our understanding of what happened? Can we pin the failure on a precise cause whose action we can trace, rigorously, through time, from before the failure to after?
2. Limit ourselves to one change that we mentally step-by-step through time, plotting its effects and their future trajectories. This deliberate precision eliminates magical thinking's error of leaping over intermediate steps. Such leaping makes outcomes seem easier than they are, leading us to overestimate a cause's power. To achieve an accurate estimate, we must slow-walk one change forward, linking actions into a causal chain.

By practicing these two techniques, we sharpen our counterfactual thinking. Once it's sharpened, it can be employed methodically when we encounter a new problem, improving our chances of finding a workable solution.

Counterfactual thinking can also be engaged before failure strikes. We can use it to anticipate hitches and perform pre-mortems, foreseeing what might go wrong so that we better prepare ourselves to respond to setbacks (or avoid them altogether).[106]

---

[103] Gopnik et al. 2001; Buchsbaum et al. 2012; Gopnik and Walker 2013; McCormack et al. 2013; Nyhout and Ganea 2019a, 2019b, 2020; Wente et al. 2022.

[104] Kahneman and Miller 1986; Kahneman 1995; Roese and Hur 1997; Roese and Olson 1997; Mandel 2003; Epstude and Roese 2007; Epstude and Roese 2011; Roese and Epstude 2017.

[105] Kahneman and Miller 1986; Roese 1997; Roese and Olson 1997; Byrne 2002; McEleney and Byrne 2006; Epstude and Roese 2011; Van Hoeck 2015; Roese and Epstude 2017.

[106] Byrne and Egan 2004; McEleney and Byrne 2006; Epstude et al. 2016; Hammell and Chan 2016; Summerville et al. 2018.

Until, at last, we achieve counterfactual thinking's three great gifts:

1. *Living in Many Futures*. This happens when our brain gets so adept at *what if* that it can perceive multiple paths ahead, all with their own special opportunities. Those paths allow us to switch courses fluently, maintaining initiative in shifting environments.

2. *Roleplaying the Outside World*. This happens when our brain develops the capacity to do *what if* not just for itself but for every actor in a situation. We can imagine the possible responses of all our friends and adversaries, teachers, and customers. We can anticipate their potential reactions to our actions. We can exist in a dynamic future, where we adapt to the world as the world adapts to us.

3. *Making the Smallest Change for the Biggest Long-Term Impact*. This happens when our brain can storythink with such slow-motion precision that it spots "butterfly effects," or in other words, the big consequences of small actions. Most small actions have small effects, but that doesn't mean that the only way to generate a big effect is with a big action. If we're rigorous in our counterfactual thinking, we can spot chances to accomplish much by changing little.

These are the gifts of novelists and screenwriters, who can envision branching tomorrows, populated with wildly different characters, each acting individually. And these are also the gifts of successful leaders, engineers, and entrepreneurs, all of whom maximize life's creative opportunity by imagining a wide range of possible futures – then devising practical paths to make dreams happen.

These gifts can be enjoyed by all of us. In Sections 8 and 9, we'll explore narrative training exercises that can have big impacts on our *why* and *what if* thinking – and with them, on our overall powers of practical imagination, real-world problem-solving, and emotional well-being.

8 Narrative Creativity Training for Students

To help students improve their narrative creativity, start with exercises that diversify their causal thinking. Then move onto exercises that sharpen their counterfactual thinking. Finally, combine the two.

The following pages contain sample exercises for all three stages. These exercises have been effective in classrooms from elementary through graduate school. They are derived from literature and theater, but instead of steering our brain to interpret or think critically about stories (as we're taught now in most literature and theater classes), they hone and extend what we do naturally when we read novels or watch dramas: roleplay, world build, and produce fan fiction, creating fresh narratives of our own.

8.1 Diversifying Causal Thinking

The purpose of the following four exercises is to increase students' mental toolbox of possible actions, giving them more varied and unique options for problem-solving and innovation.

Shift to Narrative. Pick a general source of change: kindness, intelligence, community. Then provide two narrative examples: *Jane was kind when she . . . Lee was smart when he . . . We acted as a community when we . . .*

This exercise helps students transition out of logical abstraction into narrative thinking. In logical abstraction, students equate change with timeless properties. Such properties (also known as tags, labels, and keywords) are used by computers to efficiently catalogue, search, and retrieve items, but by amalgamating individual causes into universal concepts, they shift the brain toward symbolism and magical thinking.

To reverse that shift, have students contrast their narrative examples, speculating on the causal mechanisms that distinguish one from the other. Help students see that sometimes it's kind to give people what they want and that at other times it's kind just to listen. Help them see that sometimes it can be smart to solve a problem – and sometimes smart to walk away. Help them see that community can be generated by different actors, each with their own plans and methods. The more that students run this exercise, the more that they enrich their mental catalogue of real-world causes.

Delay the Why. Select someone who acts differently than you. Seek their *why* – without asking *why.* Instead, ask: *who, where, when, what.* For example, if someone likes an activity that you don't like, ask them *who* they do it with, *where* they do it, *when* the first time they did it was, *what* they use to do it, *who* was the first person who introduced them to it, *where* was the last place they did it, and . . .

After you have gathered all the details you can, hypothesize the person's *why,* that is, their motive for acting the way they do. If the other person confirms your hypothesis, that's good. If you help the other person discover a *why* that they hadn't realized before, that's even better. You are more likely to discover a new *why* if you focus on *who, where, when, what* that surprise you, stimulating curiosity. In other words, you are more likely to find hidden causes if you focus on anomalies (see Section 7.1).

Young students can do this by interviewing each other about their favorite toys or activities. Their initial explanations may be generic: *I do it because it's fun.* Encourage deeper insight by comparing the toy or activity with similar ones – and asking *who, where, when,* and *what* they prefer about it.

Advanced students can interview people outside the classroom. And they can also focus on behaviors that they disagree with. That is, instead of simply asking about actions that prompt curiosity, they can ask about actions that incite judgment.

For these interviews to work, students must have the patience to delve at length into their interviewee's background. They must also resist the impulse to view the exercise as an opportunity to arrive at a mutual understanding, compromise, or agreement. The goal is not to identify with the other person. (Identification is a logical operation.) It is to imagine the mental mechanisms that make the other person unique, allowing the student to roleplay that person without caricature or malice.

Contrast Different Characters. Pick two (or more) people who respond differently to the same event. Resist the temptation to judge one response as better. Instead, use *Delay the Why* (see above) to search for the motives and methods (i.e., the *why* and *how*) beneath the responses, surfacing each person's unique character. Affirm the practical value of that character by imagining positive effects that it could have in other situations. What idiosyncratic insights would each person bring to a problem that you are facing now? How would the two people solve a current social or technological challenge differently from each other?

Advanced students can go beyond individuals to focus on organizations, cultures, and other collectives. They can also follow the same person through multiple situations – and track how that person's motives shift over time, revealing multiple characters inside.

The goal of this exercise is not scientific or historical accuracy. It does not matter whether students correctly identify the underlying character of the people or collectives they study. The goal is for students to diversify their own range of mental motion by discovering new possibilities to roleplay. Often, however, scientific and historical accuracy enrich the exercise, because scientific and historical accuracy press students to think beyond their assumptions and attend to the unique physical and psychological processes of outside lives.

Reverse Engineer Events. Pick an unexpected outcome or unusual effect. Work backward to unearth its unique physical or psychological cause. Focus on discovery and distinctness, resisting general rules and preexisting judgments.

Young students can do this via storybooks. Ask students to point out an interesting event in the storybook. Invite them to think about *why* it happened. To help students test their hypothesis, remove that *why* from the storybook. Does the event still occur?

Advanced students can do this with technologies, historical episodes, businesses, and so on. Research the causes carefully, resisting guesses based on analogies. The goal is to find a new action, mechanism, or intervention that can be translated to other scenarios.

8.2 Sharpening Counterfactual Thinking

The purpose of the following exercises is to help students get better at seeing the specific consequences of individual actions, in both the short-term and the long.

Rescript a Narrative. Select a story (fiction or nonfiction). Change one – and only one – thing about the story. The change could be to a character's motives or behavior. It could be to an obstacle or event. It could be an addition, subtraction, or transformation. Once the change has been made, imagine what happens next, contrasting it with the original story.

Young students can insert their friends and family into the story. Advanced students can insert distant or subtle elements: a technology, a minor character, a narrative atmosphere.

Initially, many students will focus on the immediate effects of the change, as it pertains to a single character. Challenge them to think further into the future and to attend to more characters. How will the rules of the storyworld be affected by the change? Can the student carry the change to the narrative's end – then into a sequel?

Branching Pathways. Study a situation – then hypothesize multiple events that could happen next. Avoid ranking potential outcomes as more or less likely. Entertain all possibilities, including extreme ones. But when you imagine an extreme outcome, push yourself to describe, exactly, the step-by-step of how it occurs.

Young students can do this via group Choose-Your-Own-Adventure. Begin by selecting a Choose-Your-Own-Adventure book based in history (or near-future sci-fi) that follows rules of psychology and physics relatively close to the students' lived experience. Avoid books that punish "bad" choices and reward "good" ones. Instead, opt for books with multiple positive paths of action.

Read the Choose-Your-Own-Adventure out-loud as a group, while allowing the students to make their own decisions, going on individual adventures. At each branch point, have the students choose their personal path, splitting from one another into smaller groups. Move from group to group, reading their next page. Keep the students engaged by encouraging them to listen to each other's journeys. When the book is finished, count all the positive story endings – *There are lots of worthwhile ways that life can go!*

Advanced students can author their own Choose-Your-Own-Adventures, based on real-world or near-future situations.

Go Frankenstein. Have each student select a different story. Pair up students and ask them to splice part of one story into the other. (For example, they could splice a character from the first student's story into the world of the other student's story.) Then ask: *What happens next?*

Advanced students can select two technologies or businesses to frankenstein together. Ask the students to predict the near, mid, and far future of the new hybrid.

Narrative Multiple Choice. Reimagine multiple choice. Regular multiple choice is based in logic, so it contains three wrong answers and a single right one. Narrative multiple choice contains three good answers – and a blank one that students author themselves.

For young students, pose an open-ended problem that they experience in their daily lives. Like: *How can each of us make a new classroom friend?* Offer three workable solutions. Invite the students to choose one of the solutions – or invent a fourth.

Initially, some students may be more inclined to choose an existing answer, while others may be more inclined to invent their own. But over time, as they hear each other's answers, they will come to understand that there isn't one correct path, just forking opportunities.

Advanced students can do this with more complex problems, such as business plans or technology prototypes. And they can also "break" each other's solutions, posing problems that the solution might encounter and challenging each other to respond with creative fixes.

8.3 Improving Causal and Counterfactual Thinking Together

In the brain, causal and counterfactual thinking are linked engines of creative action. The purpose of the following four exercises is to tighten the connection between causal and counterfactual thinking, using each to strengthen the other.

Perspective-Shifting. Have students partner up. Pose a real-world problem. Invite each student to privately craft their own answer. Then ask each student to tell their partner their answer and to narrate *how* they arrived at it. That narrative reveals their method, that is, their individual mechanism of problem-solving. Finally, pose a second problem – and have each student solve the problem in a way that they imagine that their partner would. In other words, have the students swap methods.

This exercise pairs explanation-seeking with speculative roleplaying. The sign of more diverse causal thinking is students who invent second-problem answers that depart from their prior method. The sign of more precise counter-factual thinking is students who better anticipate the answers of their partners.

Backwards Forwards. Introduce a character who is attempting an action. (For example, "Jane is trying to build a sandcastle.") Then, introduce an insurmount-able obstacle. (For example, "But it rains.")

Ask students to speculate on possible motives – that is, *whys* – for the character's attempted action. These speculations should not be vague or general. (For example, they should not be, "Jane wants to have fun," or "Jane wants to be happy.") Instead, like a good scientific hypothesis, they should propose a motive that is specific to the situation. (For example, "Jane wants to build a home for a queen," or "Jane wants to mold something with her hands," or "Jane wants to make something that she can destroy.")

Invite students to respond to the obstacle by suggesting alternative actions that could satisfy the hypothesized *why*. (For example, "Jane could build a home for a queen *by using blocks indoors*," or "Jane could mold something with her hands *by shaping a pot out of clay*," or "Jane could make something that she can destroy *by baking a cake and then pulling it apart to eat it*.")

Advanced students can tackle larger social or institutional problems, cre-atively navigating obstacles by backing up to see the bigger picture – before imagining new paths forward.

Roleplay Adversaries and Minor Characters. Select a story. Pick a character whom you clash with or see as peripheral. Enter the perspective of that charac-ter, searching for the character's needs and wants. Remember: Every character has their own unique needs and wants. Even comic-book villains want to rule the world in different ways for different reasons. Find those reasons by casting a wide net for eccentricities in characters' personal histories and by being specific about characters' short- and long-term goals. (In short, practice *Delay the Why*, as above.) After you've pinpointed a character's individual needs and wants, imagine that character's actions, step-by-step, as far into the future as you can go.

Young students can do this with their favorite storybooks, television series, and short-form fiction. Advanced students can do it with real-life episodes from history and even their own biographies.

This exercise helps students roleplay the entire future, with all its intersecting causes, instead of tunnel-visioning on one set of "heroic" choices and assuming that the world will passively play along.

Harnessing Conflict. Select two individuals who are in conflict. Ask students to solve a real-world problem from the perspective of one individual and then the other. Finally, ask the students to pair up the conflicting individuals and imagine how they could work together to solve the problem.

When introducing this exercise to young students, it's often helpful for one of the individuals to be the student herself. The other individual can be a parent or teacher that the student knows well.

In addition to replaying individuals, advanced students can roleplay teams or organizations who are in conflict. And they can also learn to harness their own internal conflicts. Every one of us has multiple minds inside. Usually, we feel pressed to choose between those minds, ranking one above the others. But what if we could be all our minds, together? What if, instead of seeking to resolve our inner conflict, we embraced it?

This experience of wrestling with oneself is the primordial sensation of creativity. Almost every act of invention begins with a moment of inner struggle that is gradually converted into mental flow.

———

Can you imagine how these twelve exercises will work for you or one of your specific students? Can you anticipate potential problems – and innovations?

9 Narrative Creativity Training for Working Professionals

Narrative creativity training can improve innovation, problem-solving, and leadership in working professionals.[107]

This training has been implemented at scale by the US Army, the same organization that funded the World War II research that produced ideation and AI (see Section 2). The Army's interest in the alternative approach of narrative creativity traces its origins to a 2021 research report by Angela Samosorn, a US Army Nurse Corps major who found that the Army's Professional Military Education was not effectively cultivating creative problem-solvers, planners, or strategists. Seeking a new method for training creativity, the Army's Training Command (TRADOC) reached out to the authors of this book. To develop that method, we partnered with Lieutenant Colonel Tom Gaines and US Army Special Operations, which describes its training pipeline as "roleplay with real bullets." We also worked with two Army Professors, Dr. Richard McConnell and Dr. Kenneth Long, who had academic backgrounds in Shakespeare and collaborative storytelling. The result was narrative creativity training that focused on improving innovation, leadership, and other professional tasks that require imagination.[108]

---

[107] Root-Bernstein and Root-Bernstein 2004; Nersessian 2008; Allen 2009, 2012; Lee et al. 2010; Magnani et al. 2010; Bennett and Lemoine 2014; Otis 2015; Charon 2017; Magnani 2017; Brandenburger 2019; Florida 2019; Fletcher 2023.

[108] Fletcher 2022b.

The training was independently validated by Army Special Operations and the Army's Command and General Staff College, which in 2023 awarded it a medal for "groundbreaking research." The training has been employed in hundreds of workplaces to boost problem-solving, innovation, and resilience in nurses, teachers, engineers, managers, entrepreneurs, designers, soldiers, and other professionals.[109] Here's how you can run it yourself.

9.1 Diversifying Causal Thinking

Shift to Narrative. Think of a customer, employee, product, or service. What adjective – *smart, kind, creative* – first springs to mind? Search your memory for the origin story behind the label, recalling a specific event that was *smart, kind,* or *creative.* Now forget the label, imagining what the customer, employee, product, or service does next.

Delay the Why. Make a list of difficult employees, bad patients, rogue customers, and other people who cause you anger or anxiety at work. Seek their *why* without asking *why,* instead asking *who, when, what, where.* Push beyond their initial responses to delve into their unique backstories. Don't stop until you discover a distinctively original motive for their behavior. You'll know you've discovered that motive if it expands your sense of the range of human psychology rather than falling into an existing stereotype, typology, or personality category (e.g., Myers Briggs). The person does not need to agree with your hypothesized *why* – but they must be unable to refute it. If you posit a novel motive for their behavior that they can't disprove, you've diversified your own causal thinking.

Contrast Different Characters. Select two similar technologies, products, or businesses, and unearth a single mechanism that makes them different.

Reverse Engineer Events. Select a previous-generation technology, competitor service, or business plan created by a leader, team, or organization that thinks differently than you. Rewind history to uncover the unique mechanical reasons why it worked.

9.2 Sharpening Counterfactual Thinking

Rescript a Narrative. Select a technology, service, or business plan, and change one of its elements. Don't change anything else. Envision the step-by-step effects of the single change into the future: one minute, one hour, one day, one month, one year, one decade.

---

[109] Fletcher et al. 2023.

Branching Pathways. Present your team with a work scenario. Have each member imagine three different ways that the scenario could play out, being specific about *why* and precise about *how*. Pool everyone's conjectures, highlighting unique ones and flagging common ones as instances of logical groupthink. Resist ranking certain conjectures as more or less likely. Instead, value the unlikely. Challenge your team to live in multiple tomorrows, with possible outcomes happening side-by-side.

Go Frankenstein. Have each member of your team select a favorite product or service. Pair up team members and ask each of them to spot a feature in their partner's product or service that would improve their own. Rotate partners and repeat.

Narrative Multiple Choice. Present your team with three new technologies, services, or strategies that you believe can work. Invite each team member to select one – or propose their own. Then have each team member explain why they believe that their option will succeed in the current market.

9.3 Improving Causal and Counterfactual Thinking Together

Perspective-Shifting. Have each member of your team write down how they solved a recent challenge. Partner them up to exchange stories. Then present a new problem that your organization is struggling to solve – and have each team member solve the problem from their partner's perspective.

Backwards Forwards. Select an initiative that your organization or a near-competitor has recently failed to execute. Invite your team to speculate on the deeper motives for the initiative – and to then propose alternate initiatives that would satisfy those motives.

Roleplay Adversaries and Minor Characters. Select a competitor. Study their behavior, isolating one way that they think differently than you. Adopt that way of thinking and infiltrate your own team or organization, imagining what you would change. Repeat this exercise by adopting the perspective of small start-ups, suppliers, and other minor players in your space.

Harnessing Conflict. Select two workers (or teams) with distinct, even conflicting, methods and working styles. Present them with a task or problem. Have each of them develop a solution independently. Then, pair them up and challenge them to develop a third solution that outperforms their individual ones.

9.4 Alternatives to Current Creativity Exercises

Among working professionals, the most popular creativity exercises are brainstorming, design thinking, fixation disruption, and convergent thinking. But all have shown limited long-term returns.[110] Here's how to replace them with narrative exercises that better achieve the intended effect.

Brainstorming. Brainstorming is intended to generate a rich pool of new ideas. But it suffers from drawbacks, including:

- Brainstorming sessions typically begin by asking participants to list their current challenges and opportunities. But challenges and opportunities activate fears and hopes, shifting the brain into short-term thinking and constraining its capacity for major innovation.
- Brainstorming provides an opportunity to access ideas that are already in people's heads, not a method for generating original plans.

So, instead:

- Bring together two teams with different tasks and functions. Have them swap roles. Tell them to make a plan to address each other's challenges and opportunities. Then un-swap – and challenge each team to improve the plan that the other team has proposed for them. This technique draws on narrative processes such as perspective-shifting and creative conflict. And it also leverages emotion as a motivational driver, because no team likes to think that another team can solve their problems better than they can.

Design Thinking. Design thinking is intended to make creativity more productive by targeting a specific problem and empathizing with a typical user.[111] But it suffers from drawbacks, including:

- By defining problems, it promotes troubleshooting not innovation.
- By empathizing with a typical user, it doesn't practice actual empathy. It engages in stereotyping, achieving efficiency at the expense of curiosity.

So, instead:

- Do like Charles Darwin, the nineteenth-century biologist who debunked design: root creative evolution in struggle. Start by surveying your organization, your market, or your environment for conflicting motives, mechanisms, or other causes. Don't treat the conflict between those causes as a negative to be ameliorated. Instead, treat the conflict as a creative driver by focusing on ways that the different causes can advance each other.

---

[110] Diehl and Stroebe 1987; Mullen et al. 1991; Furnham 2000; Putman and Paulus 2009; Chamorro-Premuzic 2015.
[111] Brown and Katz 2011; Kolko 2014; Lewrick et al. 2018; Brown 2019; Ney and Meinel 2019; Koskinen 2023.

- Research users who employ a product for unanticipated purposes. What insights can you gain from them about the product's latent potential?

Fixation Disruption. Fixation disruption is intended to shake us free from mental ruts by jolting the brain with random information or experiences.[112] But it suffers from drawbacks, including:

- The brain struggles to process random information and experiences, typically compartmentalizing or dismissing them.
- The brain's most original plans come when it is relaxed or in flow, not when it is confused or distracted.

So, instead:

- Research the history of the challenge you're facing and the breakthroughs of previous innovators. When researching, don't look for general rules or principles. Instead, enrich your perspective with unique events and actions, thick with specific detail.
- After you've filled your head with research, engage in a routine physical task, like jogging, knitting, or tidying. This helps activate your brain's default mode network, increasing the odds of a creative epiphany.

Convergent Thinking. Convergent thinking is intended to winnow and rank the ideas generated via brainstorming, ideation, and so on.[113] But it suffers from drawbacks, including:

- It's premised on the false assumption that creative solutions can be deduced in advance.
- It's based on past experience and is thus heavily inflected with expert bias. Its net result is to overvalue minor innovations and preclude major innovations.

So, instead:

- Gauge the novelty of the problem or opportunity that you're facing. Then venture solutions that are similarly novel, matching the newness of your plan to the newness of your situation. For example, when faced with a routine problem, go with a solution that seems reasonable to experts; when faced with a highly unusual problem, go with a solution that surprises experts but that they cannot disprove.

---

[112] Mumford et al. 2006; Storm and Angello 2010; Youmans and Arciszewski 2014; Angello et al. 2015; Crilly 2015; Vasconcelos and Crilly 2016; Alipour et al. 2018.

[113] Scott et al. 2004a, 2004b; Mumford 2001; Cropley 2006; Simonton 2015; Mumford and McIntosh 2017; Runco 2020; Zhang et al. 2020.

9.5 Overall Mentality

Organizations achieve peak performance in stable environments, where processes and products can be optimized. But such stability is fleeting. Work is inherently volatile because business involves constant competition, with customers and competitors evolving daily. To ready your organization for that volatility, automate routine tasks and processes, so that you can invest time and resources in creatively preparing for the next change.

When doing that preparation, remember:

- *The purpose of creativity training isn't to develop the plan – it's to develop the planner.* No plan survives contact with reality, but that doesn't render planning useless. Quite the opposite: by learning how to make effective plans for a wide variety of future scenarios, your team prepares itself to re-plan rapidly when the unexpected strikes.
- *Conflict, not optimization, is the source of growth.* The rich variety of biological life has been generated via the struggles of evolution by natural selection. Likewise, the rich variety of technologies, art, business services, medicines, and other cultural products has been generated by competition between inventors – and even by outright war between nations. The key to maximizing the growth of your organization is to reap more of conflict's creative benefits while minimizing its destructive consequences. Build diverse teams that thrive on difference not on agreement. Invest in red-teaming, roleplaying competitors who attack your processes.
- *Value anomalies and explanations over data.* Data perfectly predicts yesterday; anomalies reveal potential futures. Data leads to analysis paralysis; explanations drive action and insight.
- *Anchor your organization in long-term goals not in principles.* Principles (such as fairness and quality) are often framed by organizations as a way to adapt to change without sacrificing integrity. But principles are logical; when they collide with reality, they can be interpreted to fit almost any purpose. The better mechanism for maintaining organic consistency over time is to focus on long-term goals. Those goals establish the end of your organization's narrative, giving you productive flexibility in your middle chapters while providing overall consistency of direction.
- *Never treat narratives as true.* Truth is a characteristic of logic, not of narratives. Narratives can be falsifiable, possible, or useful – but they cannot be right or true. When you slip into thinking otherwise, communication becomes stale and strategy ossifies.
- *Bias is inevitable – and fruitful.* Bias is often framed by logicians as a heuristic short-cut, a mental rule of thumb that evolved to expedite

decision-making.[114] Biologically, however, bias is the slant produced by a person's character. It is evolutionarily useful not because it simplifies life into generally reliable axioms but because it promotes an alternative to the norm. It is, in other words, an instance of what Darwin referred to as the "divergence of character," making it a basis of evolution.[115] Biases shared by groups are therefore to be discounted, while biases unique to individuals are to be respected.

10 Narrative Creativity and Human Intelligence

Computer AI will never be capable of narrative creativity, no matter how good its data, futuristic its software, or quantum its architecture.

This statement may seem implausible, even foolish, given the recent buzz about LLMs. But it follows necessarily from the mechanics of computer hardware.[116] That hardware cannot perform narrative processes. Not because those processes are supernatural, but because computers are engineered to run a different physical operation: logic.

The training presented in this book's previous sections does not depend upon the material distinction between logic and narrative, and since we have explained its technicalities elsewhere,[117] we won't belabor the point here. However, the better that educational institutions grasp the technical limits of AI, the more that they can cultivate human creativity, so let's run through the key points now.

10.1 The Mechanical Difference Between Logic and Narrative

The term *logic* has a wide range of colloquial meanings that encompass just about every act of deliberative thinking that can be performed by a reasonable person. But logic could not be hardwired into computers if it did not consist of a precise set of mechanical operations. Those operations are AND/OR/NOT, which can themselves be reduced to a single operation, either NAND or NOR. (NOR gates were the sole component of the Apollo Guidance Computer that landed humans on the Moon.)[118]

This mechanical simplicity is why logic is such a useful tool. Simplicity powers scale, allowing computers to handle big data. And the same simplicity enables us to demystify AI. AI is logic, automated. Its algorithms (no matter how intricate) and its symbolic languages (no matter how abstruse) all follow the rules of logic, and those rules operate through equations. So, if you

---

[114] For example, Kahneman 2011.   [115] Darwin 1859, chapter 4.
[116] Larson 2021; Fletcher 2021a, 2022c, 2024b.
[117] Fletcher and Benveniste 2022; Fletcher 2023, 2024b, 2025.   [118] O'Brien 2010.

understand the physical mechanics of what equations can and cannot do, you know the power and the limits of AI, now and forever.

Equations exist in the eternal present tense of $X = Y$, or in other words, X *is* Y. And the present tense cannot contain action. Action consists of a cause and its effect, and a cause and its effect can't exist concurrently. A cause must materially precede its effect in time, necessitating either a past or a future (i.e., a past cause for a present effect, or a future effect for a present cause). When actions are fed into the eternal *is* of equations, those equations are thus tasked with a contradiction: *Render a cause and its effect into a present-tense instant.* Or in other words: *Take two things that can't physically coexist – and make them simultaneous.*

Computers execute this paradoxical task by converting causation into correlation, or in other words, by equating causes with their effects, such that *fire = smoke* and *smoking = cancer*. These equations may seem reasonable – after all, when there's smoke, there's typically fire, and when there's smoking, there's often cancer. But these equations are in fact magical thinking. If *fire = smoke*, then *smoke = fire*, which would mean that smoke causes fire (and that cancer causes smoking). By equating causes with effects, computers thus delete the mechanics of action, and with it, real-world physics and psychology.

The inability of computers to grasp causation is not a software limit. It is a hardware limit. It is a feature of a brain that is built, physically, from logic gates. The limit was foreseen long ago by Aristotle, formally proved by Bertrand Russell,[119] and maintained today by Judea Pearl, the inventor of causal calculus.[120] It is a practical restriction inherent to any general computing device, aka Turing machine, so it pertains to quantum computers as well.

This restriction is not disputed by AI experts. Specialists in "causal" machine learning acknowledge that logical induction (i.e., the observation of data) cannot yield causal invention (i.e., new mechanical explanations for *why* or *how*).[121] Machine learning's statistical approach can go no further than determining the probability of causal mechanisms posited by human engineering, permitting AI to test causal architectures but not invent them.[122] And although computers can run so-called "counterfactual" calculations in which a hypothetical datapoint is plugged into a mathematical model,[123] they cannot run counterfactual

---

[119] Russell 1912.   [120] Pearl 1993, 2009b.

[121] Causal AI requires its dataset to contain all possible causal variables. For Causal AI to function, domain experts must therefore structure observations as "data," and they must also supply initial causal assumptions in the form of structural causal models (SCMs). See, for example, Schölkopf et al. 2021; Schölkopf 2022.

[122] Glymour et al. 2019; Huang et al. 2020; Nogueira et al. 2022.

[123] Fernández-Loría et al. 2020; Stepin et al. 2021; Chou et al. 2022.

narratives.[124] Counterfactual narratives incorporate new causes; mathematical models can only incorporate new numbers.

Why is it, then, that LLMs can craft new stories, apparently performing narrative creativity? Why can they explain why things happen in stories, apparently performing causal narration? Why can they rewrite stories to include new events, apparently performing counterfactual narration?

The answer is: LLMs are heavily hand-coded by human engineers.[125] They are not pure AIs that teach themselves through induction, deduction, interpretation, and Bayesian statistics. They are a mix of modern AI and old-fashioned programming. That programming includes predetermined story structures that enable the LLM to re-skin conventional plots in fresh language, allowing the LLM to mimic the appearance of creative narration when it is in fact recycling narrative architectures invented by humans.

The hybrid AI-programming structure of LLMs may seem a minor quibble. Why does it matter how LLMs are doing what they are doing, so long as they are doing it? But it is of massive consequence. Programs lack the capacity for independent discovery that gives AI the practical intelligence to teach itself chess. The fact that LLMs need to be programmed with story structures reveals that they lack the capacity for independent discovery with regard to narrative. They must rely on human assistance to perform narrative invention, rendering LLMs incapable of self-sufficient scientific inquiry, technological innovation, or creative problem-solving.[126]

Large Language Models are what they state they are: language models. They deal in language, not story, and in mathematical models, not narrative

---

[124] Wu et al. 2024.   [125] Naveed et al. 2023.

[126] Current work in Causal AI is based on the premise that deep learning, LLMs, and neural net technologies are inherently associational/correlational, rendering them unable to grasp causal mechanisms or autonomously move up Judea Pearl's "ladder of causation" (see Kıcıman et al. 2023; Liu et al. 2024; Weinberg et al. 2024; Zečević et al. 2023; Jin et al. 2023; Zhou et al. 2024; Gao et al. 2023). Causal AI thus requires human data analysis and training, and although LLMs can simulate causal reasoning, they do so by recombining the language of causal insight present in training texts, prompting Pearl to observe that this is mere textual recycling and a main reason LLMs do not generalize causally (Pearl 2023). Causal AI attempts to correct this deficiency by directly encoding causal information though schema such as directed acyclic graphs (DAGs) and SCMs. From human encoded structural equations of the relationships between nodes in the model and the suspected causal variables in their distribution, Causal AI can simulate counterfactual interventions on the data, either through the creation of synthetic control sets from the extant data for comparison to the effect group, or through calculations of simulated interventions of its causal model. In theory, this allows Causal AI to test and validate causal hypotheses; identify latent or hidden causal variables/factors; and modify the knowledge represented in the DAG or SCM. All this is, however, built on top of human causal reasoning and discovery. The models rely on expert definitions of the domain and salient variables, and they rely on human knowledge for initial causal representations. For more, see Schölkopf et al. 2021; Schölkopf 2022; Jin et al. 2023; Mooij et al. 2013; Shanmugam 2018; Pearl 2009; Peters et al. 2017.

mechanisms. They can output random words that obey the logic of standard syntax, allowing them to generate verbiage that follows established patterns of speech. Yet they cannot use narrative as a tool to discover new *whys* or *hows*.[127]

But what if someday computers do what the human brain has done: achieve consciousness? Won't LLMs be capable of doing narrative then?[128]

No. Consciousness isn't the source of narrative intelligence. Many of our brain's narrative operations are nonconscious, which is why athletes can innovate new actions spontaneously and why fresh plans often seem to pop into our mind from nowhere.[129] The claim that consciousness will make computers capable of casual discovery is magical thinking. It jumps from a cause (consciousness) to an effect (narrative intelligence) without describing the step-by-step mechanism that connects the two.

10.2 The Human Task Ahead

The shortcomings of current AI are typically seen either as a challenge for computer programmers or as a triumph for humanity. They are neither.

No programmer will engineer a computer AI that can perform a fraction of human creativity. Because computer hardware can't run narrative, AI will never be capable of innovation, creative problem-solving, original strategy, or visionary leadership. It is limited to ideating text, images, and other symbol systems. Yet this doesn't mean that we humans can kick back and declare victory. It means that we need to move fast to reshape our relationship to AI.

First, we are investing in AI to replace human creatives. By doing so, we are abandoning our duty of care to our communities. It is negligent to offload responsibility for our future onto algorithms that cannot plan, strategize, or innovate. It is unethical to expect computers to cure cancer and anxiety, or to fix poverty and partisanship.[130] If we want to solve humanity's problems, we must do so ourselves.

---

[127] Tian et al. 2023.

[128] Kurzweil 2000; Husain 2017; Levesque 2018; Gawdat 2022; Brachman and Levesque 2022.

[129] Bargh et al. 2001; Imanaka et al. 2002; Eitam et al. 2008; Hassin et al. 2009; Tan et al. 2015; Abraham 2018; Fox and Beaty 2019; Teng and Lien 2022; Aru et al. 2023.

[130] The vast majority of current computational approaches to innovation and creativity aim to replicate either artistic creativity or industrial innovation. The former emphasizes novelty over utility; the latter occurs in well-defined technical fields with high degrees of (presumed) causal regularity (e.g., molecular pharmacology, precision agriculture, economic analysis and decision making, structural engineering, geology). These application domains cluster at two poles of the causal spectrum: idiosyncratic, individual creativity in which constrained randomness approximates non-obvious innovation; and exhaustive iteration and statistical evaluation in domains with prescribed causal structures. Overlooked in the middle of the two poles are the many problem domains (e.g., politics, economics, business, pedagogy) that don't admit of clearly deterministic causal models or whose data are subjective (or theory dependent), in no small part because they include humans as causal agents, interacting unpredictably. The creative solutions

Second, we are training our brains – and our children – to think like AI. We are turning our schools into machines for drilling students in memorization, math, deduction, logic puzzles, critical thinking, interpretation, ideation, and other computational processes. We are converting our healthcare systems, businesses, and governments into systems that use metric assessments, Lean management, and spreadsheets to promote efficiency, fairness, and optimization. All of which is mathematically ideal – but dangerously frail in real-world volatility.

Is it any surprise that our minds are now suffering from AI's shortcomings: the brittleness, the shallow imagination, the brute force problem-solving? Or, that our classrooms and workplaces are awash with the conviction that there are *right* answers (aka, optimum solutions) even as they become less rich with *new* answers? Or, that we're finding ourselves increasingly unable to cope with life's usual setbacks, as our brains short circuit with anger, intolerance, and anxiety?

To reverse these trends, we must invest more in human intelligence, nurturing children's natural creativity and deliberately improving the adult brain's narrative capacities to diversify *why* and sharpen *what if*. The previous sections have outlined what we can do, right now, to start. The next, and final, section will imagine future steps.

11 Advanced Practices for the Future

At the end of the nineteenth century, medicine evolved. It set aside the eminently logical but practically ineffective method of induction and deduction upon which it had relied for thousands of years, and it embraced a patient-centered, empirical approach that valued experiment, discovery, and growth. It stopped treating patients as lists of symptoms to be probabilistically interpreted. It started making fresh hypotheses about *why* people got sick and *how* they could be cured. It replaced old ideas about leeches and dangerous smells with germ theory, sterilization, and blood transfusions.

What was done with medicine, we have the opportunity to do with creativity. Creativity seems to us largely a mystery, just as healthcare did in the late nineteenth century. We possess a few tools for coaxing out its potential, yet for the most part, human imagination remains a black box, barely removed from the occult wonder that the ancients worshipped.

We cannot change this via iterative improvements to current theory and practice. We need to revisit the basics, thinking deeply about *why* we are struggling to be creative – and *what if* we did different.

---

and innovations required by such human-domain problems are not limited to tweaks or extrapolations of existing paradigms; they require transformations of existing causal models.

11.1 Why Do We Get Less Creative in School?

School today is the result of logical reforms whose well-meaning purpose is to be meritocratic (see Section 4). This noble aspiration has, however, proved frequently counterproductive. By emphasizing fairness and truth, school today tends toward standardization,[131] excluding flexibility and gravitating toward ranking: *top ten percent, B+, valedictorian.*[132] This nurtures unhealthy conflict, making life zero-sum instead of symbiotic. It breeds anxiety, anger, and self-silencing. And it impedes creativity. The more that a student believes that there is a right answer, the less likely she is to venture a *new* answer, making her more likely to give up, get aggressive, or submit to authority.

The alternative is straightforward. Instead of assessing students with true–false tests, give them open-ended problems without a single right solution. If you're a teacher, don't ask questions to which you already know the answer. Instead, partner with students in genuine inquiry, posing questions that you can explore together. Otherwise, your questions aren't real questions. They're a power play.

We can achieve this educational shift by front-and-centering students' problems in the classroom. Instead of trying to imprint students with what we believe they should learn, we can invite them to bring in their own questions, requiring us to search with them for new tools and solutions. Once we gain students' trust and enthusiasm, we can then help them improve their narrative creativity. We can introduce them to the techniques of causal thinking, guiding them to see the questions beneath their questions. And we can mentor them in counterfactual thinking, showing them how to invent new opportunities for action – and how to measure the effects via real-world experiments.

This training nurtures curiosity, empathy, self-efficacy, and resilience. And it can open modern schools to overlooked or undervalued ways of thinking, including the following.

11.2 Low-Data Intelligence

The human brain can be very smart with very little information. The human brain is not *always* smart with very little information. But the fact that it *can* be smart reveals that the answer is not necessarily more facts. Often, the way ahead lies in noticing anomalies, quirks, and other forms of exceptional information.

---

[131] García 2014; Alismail and McGuire 2015; Dixon-Román 2017; Koretz 2017; Tampio 2018; Wai and Lakin 2020.

[132] Anderson and Cohen 2018; Baird and Elliott 2018; Volchik and Maslyukova 2018; Tampio 2018; Muller 2019; Beach 2021.

Exceptional information is an exception to one of our mental rules of action. It exposes the rule as insufficient, revealing that there are more *hows* and *whys* to be made or discovered.

Exceptional information is everywhere, yet the longer we go through life, the worse we get at spotting it. Adults notice less exceptional information than children do, and experts less than novices. Which is fine when our mental rules are working, but no good when those rules are out of sync with our environment.

11.3 Healthy Struggle

Struggle is viewed by logic as evidence of a mistake or a bad actor: If people disagree, one of them must be ignorant – or intentionally malicious. Logic therefore dictates that we sanitize our schools and workplaces of clashing lifestyles, methods, and purposes. To logic, truth is not contested; it is harmonious.

This emphasis on harmony is divorced from life. And it smothers creativity. Struggle is the engine of biological growth and evolution. And it is also a driver of invention: rare is the creator who sits down and rationally deduces the future. Frequent is the creator who wrestles with herself and her world.

If we want more creativity in our schools and workplaces, we must get comfortable with conflict. Not conflict in the sense of a zero-sum contest to crown a winner. But conflict in the sense of curious engagement with radically different ways of thinking and acting.

We must see difference as an opportunity to learn and to listen. We must dispense with the idea that the purpose of conversation is to find compromises or areas of agreement. It is better, for all of us, if we do not agree, if we become sharper in our differences the more that we exchange them.

Differences power innovation. Eliminate them, whether through exclusion, segregation, or synthesis, and growth slows and life withers. Embrace them and we learn to take joy in variety, to develop calm resilience to challenges, and to cherish the uniqueness of ourselves and everyone around.

11.4 Process Recognition – Not Pattern Recognition

Logic excels at identifying patterns. But patterns are the gateway to symbolism and magical thinking. They return us to the science of the Middle Ages, when physics was semiotic.

Life's actual driver is mechanical processes. Processes cannot be deduced from data. They must be intuited from rogue events. Those events spark our brain to coin *why* hypotheses, which we can then test via *what-if* experiments. Such experiments can never verify that a hypothesis is true (i.e., they can never prove that the process really exists). But the more that experiments fail to falsify a hypothesis, the more confidence that we can place in it.

Because our brain is born with the narrative equipment to run causal and counterfactual thinking, it can engage in process recognition. Computers cannot. When we rely on AI and big data, we lose contact with the material mechanisms that enable us to remake reality.

11.5 A New Humanities

The humanities have fallen out of favor because the training they offer now is redundant. It consists of critical thinking, interpretation, and other logic-based skills that can be taught more efficiently in psychology, economics, and computer science courses.

But the humanities don't need to be redundant. They're rich with resources for nurturing causal and counterfactual thinking, which is to say, for stimulating imaginative problem-solving and major innovation. There's a reason that scientists and inventors have a long history of reading speculative fiction, from sci-fi to Shakespeare. And our global library abounds with other narrative art – literature, memoir, historical chronicles, painting, sculpture, dance – that can grow our brain's powers of invention in ways that logic can't.

A New Humanities could unlock those powers by pivoting toward neuroscience and narrative theory, enriching our brain's library of *whys* and its power to invent new *hows*.

11.6 The Brain's Creative Switch

Creativity is smart. Except, when it isn't. It's not smart to get creative when doing routine surgery, airplane maintenance, or safety engineering.

Creativity is intelligent only when we encounter a new problem or have the opportunity to innovate. Creativity is counterproductive (and often destructive) when a plan is working or there isn't leeway for experiment. Which is why creativity isn't to be encouraged all the time. It's not to be celebrated as an automatic good, an intrinsic virtue. It is, like everything in our brain, a tool. There are occasions when creativity is helpful and other times when it generates new problems or makes existing problems worse.

To get the most out of creativity, we thus must do more than learn to improve it. We must get faster at targeting *when* to use it and *how* to toggle it on and off. Children struggle to shut it down. Most adults struggle to turn it up. And almost all of us struggle over when to use it.

We can do better. Our brain comes equipped with an onboard sensor system – our emotions – to guide us into knowing *when* and *how* to transition into creativity. Anger and anxiety are cues that it's time to get creative. Curiosity and empathy are helpful transitioners.

The more we learn about our emotions, the better we can get at flipping our creative switch.

11.7 Partnering Logical and Narrative Creativity

The problem with modern business and education isn't logic – it's an over-emphasis on logic. We've made the mistake of thinking that if some is good, more must be optimum.

Because logic is useful, the cure for our twenty-first century can't be found by eliminating logic. To maximize our creativity, we need to establish schools and businesses that do what our brain does naturally: treat logic and narrative as complementary.

As of now, we know very little about how logical and narrative creativity training can be integrated. But the evidence we have suggests that they can be fruitfully combined.[133] The challenge for our future is to deepen our understanding of how these two very different processes can grow each other, so that we resist the urge to repeat our current mistake of preferring one and instead explore ways to couple their distinct actions, generating opportunities for new gains.

Coda: Distinguishing Logic from Narrative

Logic	Narrative
Design	Plan
Meaning	Purpose
Pattern	Process
Deduce	Infer
Sign	Effect
Reason	Science
Probability	Possibility
Semantics	Rhetoric
If–then	Causation
Interpret	Hypothesize
Concept	Action
Critical thinking	Commonsense
Principle	Method

---

[133] Fletcher 2024a.

(cont.)

Logic	Narrative
Ideation	Imagination
Truth	History
Data	Events
Algorithm	Mechanism
Archetype	Character
Symbol	Power
Math	Physics
Language	Literature
Theme	Story
Model	Storyworld
Context	Environment
Sense-making	Use-making
Efficiency	Effectiveness

In daily speech, the terms on the left are frequently conflated with those on the right. This conflation is possible because the human brain possesses both logical and narrative faculties.

But the blurring of logic and narrative has negative consequences when we train logic and expect improvement at planning, imagination, commonsense, scientific thinking, and other narrative processes, as we're now doing in modern schools and workplaces.

Appendix: Assessing Narrative Creativity

Can creativity be assessed? Can teachers determine when students are imagining with greater dynamism? Can organizations spot which strategies are more fundamentally inventive?

The answer is: yes. But you can be forgiven if you feel some skepticism.

One good reason for skepticism is that creativity generates the new. And the new can't be measured by existing yardsticks. The new, by its nature, exceeds past experience. Nothing premade – including assessments – can capture it completely.

Another good reason for skepticism is the underwhelming performance of many standard assessments of creativity. Those assessments are based on logic, which tries to quantify creativity either (1) by counting the number of ideas produced during a brainstorm or (2) by computing the divergence between an idea's elements. The limitation of the first approach is that quantity is not synonymous with quality. A lone plan can be wildly novel, while a billion others can be clichéd. The limitation of the second approach is that it's pegged to existing idea systems. It treats creativity as intrinsic and conceptual, excluding the practical and mechanical, two major drivers of real-world innovation.

These reasons for skepticism about creativity assessment are valid. But they can be addressed by the Consensual Assessment Technique, or CAT. Invented in the 1980s and validated through thousands of studies, the CAT convenes a panel of experts, each of whom scores the creativity of a particular plan or product on a range from 0 to 10.[134]

This is not a foolproof method of assessment. It depends on the quality of the judges. And one quality, above all, is crucial for a CAT judge: subject matter expertise. If the creative product is a sonnet, it should be judged by experts in poetry. If the creative plan is a blueprint for a bridge, it should be judged by experts in civil engineering. Without that expertise, it's impossible to gauge originality. A civil engineer might incorrectly see creativity in a sonnet that an expert in poetry would recognize instantly as highly derivative.

As necessary as expertise is for a CAT judge, however, expertise poses a potential danger to creativity: expert bias. Expert bias is a skew toward your

---

[134] Amabile 1982; Kaufman et al. 2007, 2008; Baer and Kaufmann 2019; Cseh and Jeffries 2019; Plucker et al. 2019; Baer 2020.

own experience. It makes experts think that they know more than they do – and it also makes them distrustful of the unfamiliar.[135]

This distrust is why experts have a tendency to suppress new plans and products. To the expert, those new plans and products appear risky, even ridiculous. Although experts are necessary for evaluating creativity, they thus need to be handled with caution. If an expert is presented with a minor innovation, he will often rank it as being very high in creativity. Why? Well, because it looks like previous innovations that he has seen, causing him to overrate its ingenuity. Meanwhile, if an expert is presented with a major innovation, he will often insist that it isn't creative – it's crazy.

To address these problems, the traditional CAT must be modified to mitigate expert bias.[136] Instead of asking the expert panel to judge whether something is creative, the modified CAT asks two subtler questions:

> *How surprising did you find this invention? Rate your surprise from 0 to 10.*
>
> *How confident are you that this invention will succeed at its intended function? If you're confident that the invention has a low chance of succeeding, rate it a 0. If you're confident that the invention has a high chance of succeeding, give it a 10. If you're not sure whether the invention will succeed or not, give it a 5. (So, if you're somewhat sure that the invention won't succeed, rate it a 2. If you have no real clue whether the invention will succeed but think it's a little more likely to succeed than to fail, rate it a 6.)*

The second question may take experts a few moments to grasp. But once experts have learned to use the modified CAT, it leverages their past experience to measure both raw creativity and potential innovation.

Raw creativity is assessed by the first question on the modified CAT. If a plan or product surprises an expert, it has no precedent. It lies outside past experience, making it new. So, the higher that a plan or product scores on the first question, the more creative it is.

Potential innovation is assessed by the second question on the modified CAT. If an expert is confident that a plan or product won't work, then it contradicts past experience, giving it low potential for innovation. If an expert is confident that a plan or product will work, then it's in line with past experience, so it has some potential for innovation. If an expert has no idea whether a plan or product will work, then it lies outside known experience, so it has high potential for innovation: It could reveal a whole new area for research and development. So, the closer that a plan or product scores to 0 on the second question, the more

---

[135] Licuanan et al. 2007; Kaufman et al. 2009; Simonton 2013; Acar et al. 2017; Tsao et al. 2019; Fedyk and Xu 2021; Anderson et al. 2023; Yang et al. 2023.
[136] Fletcher 2022a.

likely it is to be magical thinking. The closer that a plan or product scores to 10 on the second question, the more likely that it is to be a minor innovation. The closer that a plan or product scores to 5 on the second question, the more likely it is to be a major innovation, aka, a revolution.

If it isn't feasible to run a CAT, it's possible to assess narrative creativity by measuring second-order effects such as optimism, self-efficacy, and resilience. But the most reliable way to gauge narrative creativity is with the modified CAT. Like creativity, the modified CAT takes time and effort. Which can be costly in the short term yet is worth it in the long.

References

Abraham, Anna. 2016. "The Imaginative Mind." *Human Brain Mapping* 37 (11): 4197–11. https://doi.org/10.1002/hbm.23300.

——— 2018. "The Wandering Mind: Where Imagination Meets Consciousness." *Journal of Consciousness Studies* 25 (11–12): 34–52.

Abraham, Anna, and D. Yves von Cramon. 2009. "Reality = Relevance? Insights from Spontaneous Modulations of the Brain's Default Network When Telling Apart Reality from Fiction." *PLOS ONE* 4 (3): e4741. https://doi.org/10.1371/journal.pone.0004741.

Acar, Selcuk, Cyndi Burnett, and John F. Cabra. 2017. "Ingredients of Creativity: Originality and More." *Creativity Research Journal* 29 (2): 133–44. https://doi.org/10.1080/10400419.2017.1302776.

Alipour, Leyla, Mohsen Faizi, Asghar Mohammad Moradi, and Gholamreza Akrami. 2018. "A Review of Design Fixation: Research Directions and Key Factors." *International Journal of Design Creativity and Innovation* 6 (1–2): 22–35. https://doi.org/10.1080/21650349.2017.1320232.

Alismail, Halah Ahmed, and Patrick McGuire. 2015. "21st Century Standards and Curriculum: Current Research and Practice." *Journal of Education and Practice* 6 (6): 150–54.

Allen, Charles D. 2009. *Creative Thinking for Individuals and Teams: An Essay on Creative Thinking for Military Professionals*. Carlisle Barracks, PA: US Army War College.

——— 2012. *Creative Thinking for Senior Leaders: An Essay on Creative Thinking for Military Professionals*. Carlisle Barracks, PA: US Army War College.

Alvarez, Aubry L., and Amy E. Booth. 2015. "Preschoolers Prefer to Learn Causal Information." *Frontiers in Psychology* 6: 127756.

Amabile, Teresa M. 1982. "Social Psychology of Creativity: A Consensual Assessment Technique." *Journal of Personality and Social Psychology* 43 (5): 997–1013.

Anderson, Gary L., and Michael Ian Cohen. 2018. *The New Democratic Professional in Education: Confronting Markets, Metrics, and Managerialism*. New York: Teachers College Press, Columbia University.

Anderson, Ross C., Ronald A. Beghetto, Vlad Glăveanu, and Marina Basu. 2023. "Is Curiosity Killed by the CAT? A Divergent, Open-Ended, and Generative (DOG) Approach to Creativity Assessment." *Creativity Research Journal* 35 (3): 380–95. https://doi.org/10.1080/10400419 .2022.2157588.

Angello, Genna, Benjamin C. Storm, and Steven M. Smith. 2015. "Overcoming Fixation with Repeated Memory Suppression." *Memory* 23 (3): 381–89. https://doi.org/10.1080/09658211.2014.889167.

Aru, Jaan, Moritz Drüke, Juhan Pikamäe, and Matthew E. Larkum. 2023. "Mental Navigation and the Neural Mechanisms of Insight." *Trends in Neurosciences* 46 (2): 100–109. https://doi.org/10.1016/j.tins.2022.11.002.

Asteriti, Sabrina, Sten Grillner, and Lorenzo Cangiano. 2015. "A Cambrian Origin for Vertebrate Rods," edited by Jeremy Nathans. *eLife* 4: e07166. https://doi.org/10.7554/eLife.07166.

Baer, John. 2015. *Domain Specificity of Creativity*. London: Elsevier Academic Press.

———. 2020. "The Consensual Assessment Technique." In *Handbook of Research Methods on Creativity*, edited by Viktor Dörfler and Stierand Marc, 166–177. Cheltenham, UK: Edward Elgar Publishing. https://www.elgar online.com/view/edcoll/9781786439642/9781786439642.00020.xml.

Baer, John, and J. Kaufmann. 2019. "Assessing Creativity with the Consensual Assessment Technique." In *The Palgrave Handbook of Social Creativity Research*, edited by Izabela Lebuda, and Vlad Petre Glăveanu, 27–37. Cham: Palgrave Macmillan.

Baird, Jo-Anne, and Victoria Elliott. 2018. "Metrics in Education – Control and Corruption." *Oxford Review of Education* 44 (5): 533–44. https://doi.org/10.1080/03054985.2018.1504858.

Barbot, Baptiste, Todd I. Lubart, and Maud Besançon. 2016. "'Peaks, Slumps, and Bumps': Individual Differences in the Development of Creativity in Children and Adolescents." *New Directions for Child and Adolescent Development* 2016 (151): 33–45. https://doi.org/10.1002/cad.20152.

Bargh, John A., Peter M. Gollwitzer, Annette Lee-Chai, Kimberly Barndollar, and Roman Trötschel. 2001. "The Automated Will: Nonconscious Activation and Pursuit of Behavioral Goals." *Journal of Personality and Social Psychology* 81 (6): 1014–27.

Basch, Samantha, and Su-hua Wang. 2024. "Causal Learning by Infants and Young Children: From Computational Theories to Language Practices." *WIREs Cognitive Science*, April, e1678. https://doi.org/10.1002/wcs.1678.

Beach, J. M. 2021. *The Myths of Measurement and Meritocracy: Why Account ability Metrics in Higher Education Are Unfair and Increase Inequality*. New York: Rowman & Littlefield.

Beaty, Roger E., Dan R. Johnson, Daniel C. Zeitlen, and Boris Forthmann. 2022. "Semantic Distance and the Alternate Uses Task: Recommendations for Reliable Automated Assessment of Originality." *Creativity Research Journal* 34 (3): 245–60. https://doi.org/10.1080/10400419.2022.2025720.

Belski, Iouri, and Regina Belski. 2018. "Are We Fit to Graduate Creative Professionals?" In *2018 IEEE International Conference on Teaching, Assessment, and Learning for Engineering (TALE)*, 365–71. Wollongong, NSW, Australia: Institute of Electrical and Electronics Engineers. https://doi.org/10.1109/TALE.2018.8615357.

Benedek, Mathias, and Aljoscha C. Neubauer. 2013. "Revisiting Mednick's Model on Creativity-Related Differences in Associative Hierarchies: Evidence for a Common Path to Uncommon Thought." *The Journal of Creative Behavior* 47 (4): 273–89. https://doi.org/10.1002/jocb.35.

Bennett, Nate, and G. James Lemoine. 2014. "What VUCA Really Means for You." *Harvard Business Review* 92: 27.

Bergey, Claire, Benjamin Morris, and Daniel Yurovsky. 2020. "Children Hear More about What Is Atypical than What Is Typical." PsyArXiv. https://doi.org/10.31234/osf.io/5wvu8.

Bhaskar, Roy. 2020. *A Realist Theory of Science*. Radical Thinkers. New York: Verso.

Bilbao, Imanol, and Javier Bilbao. 2017. "Overfitting Problem and the Over-Training in the Era of Data: Particularly for Artificial Neural Networks." In *2017 Eighth International Conference on Intelligent Computing and Information Systems (ICICIS)*, 173–77. Cairo: Institute of Electrical and Electronics Engineers (IEEE).

Boden, Margaret A. 1996. "Chapter 9 – Creativity." In *Artificial Intelligence*, edited by Margaret A. Boden, 267–91. Handbook of Perception and Cognition. San Diego: Academic Press. https://doi.org/10.1016/B978-012161964-0/50011-X.

———. 2004. *The Creative Mind: Myths and Mechanisms*. New York: Routledge.

Brachman, Ronald J., and Hector J. Levesque. 2022. *Machines Like Us: Toward AI with Common Sense*. Cambridge, MA: MIT Press.

Brandenburger, Adam. 2019. "Strategy Needs Creativity." *Harvard Business Review* 97 (2): 59–66.

Bridgeman, Teresa. 2005. "Thinking Ahead: A Cognitive Approach to Prolepsis." *Narrative* 13 (2): 125–59. https://doi.org/10.1353/nar.2005.0007.

Broekhoven, Kim van, Barbara Belfi, Ian Hocking, and Rolf van der Velden. 2020. "Fostering University Students' Idea Generation and Idea Evaluation Skills with a Cognitive-Based Creativity Training." *Creativity: Theories – Research – Applications* 7 (2): 284–308. https://doi.org/10.2478/ctra-2020-0015.

Brogaard, Berit. 2011. "Conscious Vision for Action versus Unconscious Vision for Action?" *Cognitive Science* 35 (6): 1076–104. https://doi.org/10.1111/j.1551-6709.2011.01171.x.

Brooks, Peter. 1992. *Reading for the Plot: Design and Intention in Narrative*. Cambridge, MA: Harvard University Press.

Brown, Tim. 2019. *Change by Design, Revised and Updated: How Design Thinking Transforms Organizations and Inspires Innovation*. New York: HarperCollins.

Brown, Tim, and Barry Katz. 2011. "Change by Design." *Journal of Product Innovation Management* 28 (3): 381–83. https://doi.org/10.1111/j.1540-5885 .2011.00806.x.

Brucks, Melanie S., and Szu-Chi Huang. 2020. "Does Practice Make Perfect? The Contrasting Effects of Repeated Practice on Creativity." *Journal of the Association for Consumer Research* 5 (3): 291–301. https://doi.org/ 10.1086/709174.

Buchsbaum, Daphna, Sophie Bridgers, Deena Skolnick Weisberg, and Alison Gopnik. 2012. "The Power of Possibility: Causal Learning, Counterfactual Reasoning, and Pretend Play." *Philosophical Transactions of the Royal Society B: Biological Sciences* 367 (1599): 2202–12. https:// doi.org/10.1098/rstb.2012.0122.

Budd, Graham E., and Illiam S. C. Jackson. 2016. "Ecological Innovations in the Cambrian and the Origins of the Crown Group Phyla." *Philosophical Transactions of the Royal Society B-Biological Sciences* 371 (1685): 12. https://doi.org/10.1098/rstb.2015.0287.

Bycroft, Michael. 2012. "Psychology, Psychologists, and the Creativity Movement: The Lives of Method Inside and Outside the Cold War." In *Cold War Social Science: Knowledge Production, Liberal Democracy, and Human Nature*, edited by Mark Solovey, and Hamilton Cravens, 197–214. New York: Palgrave Macmillan. https://doi.org/10.1057/9781137013224_11.

Byrne, Ruth M. J. 2002. "Mental Models and Counterfactual Thoughts about What Might Have Been." *Trends in Cognitive Sciences* 6 (10): 426–31. https://doi.org/10.1016/S1364-6613(02)01974-5.

2016. "Counterfactual Thought." *Annual Review of Psychology* 67 (1): 135–57. https://doi.org/10.1146/annurev-psych-122414-033249.

Byrne, Ruth M. J., and Suzanne M. Egan. 2004. "Counterfactual and Prefactual Conditionals." *Canadian Journal of Experimental Psychology/Revue Canadienne de Psychologie Expérimentale* 58 (2): 113–20. https://doi.org/ 10.1037/h0085791.

Callanan, Maureen A., and Lisa M. Oakes. 1992. "Preschoolers' Questions and Parents' Explanations: Causal Thinking in Everyday Activity." *Cognitive Development* 7 (2): 213–33. https://doi.org/10.1016/0885-2014(92)90012-G.

Campbell, John. 2020. *Causation in Psychology.* Cambridge, MA: Harvard University Press.

Campbell-Kelly, Martin, William Aspray, Nathan Ensmenger, and Jeffrey R. Yost. 2013. *Computer: A History of the Information Machine*, 3rd ed. Boulder, CO: Westview Press.

Carnovalini, Filippo, and Antonio Rodà. 2020. "Computational Creativity and Music Generation Systems: An Introduction to the State of the Art." *Frontiers in Artificial Intelligence* 3: 14. https://doi.org/10.3389/frai .2020.00014.

Carroll, Joseph. 2020. "Imagination, the Brain's Default Mode Network, and Imaginative Verbal Artifacts." In *Evolutionary Perspectives on Imaginative Culture*, edited by Joseph Carroll, Mathias Clasen, and Emelie Jonsson, 31–52. Cham: Springer International. https://doi.org/10.1007/978-3-030-46190-4_2.

Carroll, Noël. 2001. "On the Narrative Connection." In *New Perspectives on Narrative Perspective*, 21–41. Albany, NY: State University of New York Press.

Cartwright, Nancy. 1979. "Causal Laws and Effective Strategies." *Nous*, (13): 419–37.

2002. *Nature's Capacities and Their Measurement.* Reprint. Oxford: Clarendon Press.

2007. *Hunting Causes and Using Them: Approaches in Philosophy and Economics.* Cambridge, UK: Cambridge University Press.

ed. 2016. *Rethinking Order: After the Laws of Nature.* London: Bloomsbury Academic, an imprint of Bloomsbury.

Cassotti, Mathieu, Anaëlle Camarda, Nicolas Poirel, Olivier Houdé, and Marine Agogué. 2016. "Fixation Effect in Creative Ideas Generation: Opposite Impacts of Example in Children and Adults." *Thinking Skills and Creativity* 19 (March): 146–52. https://doi.org/10.1016/j.tsc.2015.10.008.

Center for the New Economy and Society. 2018. "World Economic Forum: The Future of Jobs Report 2018." World Economic Forum. www3.weforum .org/docs/WEF_Future_of_Jobs_2018.pdf.

2020. "World Economic Forum: The Future of Jobs Report 2020." World Economic Forum. www3.weforum.org/docs/WEF_Future_of_Jobs_2018 .pdf.

2023. "World Economic Forum: The Future of Jobs Report 2023." World Economic Forum. www3.weforum.org/docs/WEF_Future_of_Jobs_2018 .pdf.

Chamorro-Premuzic, Tomas. 2015. "Why Group Brainstorming Is a Waste of Time." *Harvard Business Review*, March 25, 2015. https://hbr.org/2015/ 03/why-group-brainstorming-is-a-waste-of-time.

Chappell, Kerry, Teresa Cremin, and Robert Jeffrey. 2015. *Creativity, Education and Society: Writings of Anna Craft*. Edited by Kerry Chappell, Teresa Cremin, and Robert Jeffrey. London: Trentham Books. www.ucl-ioe-press.com/books/schools-and-schooling/creativity-education-and-society/.

Charon, Rita. 2017. *The Principles and Practice of Narrative Medicine*. Oxford, UK: Oxford University Press.

Chen, Liuqing, Pan Wang, Hao Dong, et al. 2019. "An Artificial Intelligence Based Data-Driven Approach for Design Ideation." *Journal of Visual Communication and Image Representation* 61: 10–22. https://doi.org/10.1016/j.jvcir.2019.02.009.

Cheng, Patricia W., and Marc J. Buehner. 2012. "Causal Learning." In *The Oxford Handbook of Thinking and Reasoning*, 210–33. Oxford, UK: Oxford University Press.

Cheung, Chau-Kiu, Elisabeth Rudowicz, Xiaodong Yue, and Anna S. F. Kwan. 2003. "Creativity of University Students: What Is the Impact of Field and Year of Study?" *The Journal of Creative Behavior* 37 (1): 42–63. https://doi.org/10.1002/j.2162-6057.2003.tb00825.x.

Chou, Yu-Liang, Catarina Moreira, Peter Bruza, Chun Ouyang, and Joaquim Jorge. 2022. "Counterfactuals and Causability in Explainable Artificial Intelligence: Theory, Algorithms, and Applications." *Information Fusion* 81: 59–83.

Chylińska, Monika, and Arkadiusz Gut. 2020. "Pretend Play as a Creative Action: On the Exploratory and Evaluative Features of Children's Pretense." *Theory & Psychology* 30 (4): 548–66. https://doi.org/10.1177/0959354320931594.

Coleman, Emma, Tripp Shealy, Jacob Grohs, and Allison Godwin. 2020. "Design Thinking among First-Year and Senior Engineering Students: A Cross-Sectional, National Study Measuring Perceived Ability." *Journal of Engineering Education* 109 (1): 72–87. https://doi.org/10.1002/jee.20298.

Craft, Anna. 2004. "Little c Creativity." In *Creativity in Education*, edited by Anna Craft, reprinted, 45–61. London: Continuum.

———. 2015. "Possibility Thinking: From What Is to What Might Be." In *The Routledge International Handbook of Research on Teaching Thinking*, edited by Rupert Wegerif and Li Li, 153–57. London: Routledge.

Craft, Anna, Teresa Cremin, Pamela Burnard, Tatjana Dragovic, and Kerry Chappell. 2013. "Possibility Thinking: Culminative Studies of an Evidence-Based Concept Driving Creativity?" *Education 3-13* 41 (5): 538–56. https://doi.org/10.1080/03004279.2012.656671.

Craft, Anna, and Kerry Anne Chappell. 2016. "Possibility Thinking and Social Change in Primary Schools." *Education 3-13* 44 (4): 407–25. https://doi.org/10.1080/03004279.2014.961947.

Cremin, Teresa, ed. 2017. *Storytelling in Early Childhood: Enriching Language, Literacy and Classroom Culture*. London: Routledge.

Cremin, Teresa, Kerry Chappell, and Anna Craft. 2013. "Reciprocity between Narrative, Questioning and Imagination in the Early and Primary Years: Examining the Role of Narrative in Possibility Thinking." *Thinking Skills and Creativity* 9 (August): 135–51. https://doi.org/10.1016/j.tsc.2012.11.003.

Crilly, Nathan. 2015. "Fixation and Creativity in Concept Development: The Attitudes and Practices of Expert Designers." *Design Studies* 38 (May): 54–91. https://doi.org/10.1016/j.destud.2015.01.002.

Cropley, Arthur. 2006. "In Praise of Convergent Thinking." *Creativity Research Journal* 18 (3): 391–404. https://doi.org/10.1207/s15326934crj1803_13.

Cropley, David H. 2015. "Promoting Creativity and Innovation in Engineering Education." *Psychology of Aesthetics, Creativity, and the Arts* 9: 161–71. https://doi.org/10.1037/aca0000008.

Cseh, Genevieve M., and Karl K. Jeffries. 2019. "A Scattered CAT: A Critical Evaluation of the Consensual Assessment Technique for Creativity Research." *Psychology of Aesthetics, Creativity, and the Arts* 13 (2): 159–66. https://doi .org/10.1037/aca0000220.

Darwin, Charles. 1859. *On the Origin of Species by Natural Selection*. London: John Murray.

Davidson, Donald. 1963. "Actions, Reasons, and Causes." *The Journal of Philosophy* 60 (23): 685–700. https://doi.org/10.2307/2023177.

1967. "Causal Relations." *The Journal of Philosophy* 64 (21): 691–703. https://doi.org/10.2307/2023853.

Deng, Lih-Yuan, and Dennis K. J. Lin. 2000. "Random Number Generation for the New Century." *The American Statistician* 54 (2): 145–50. https://doi .org/10.2307/2686034.

Diehl, Michael, and Wolfgang Stroebe. 1987. "Productivity Loss in Brainstorming Groups: Toward the Solution of a Riddle." *Journal of Personality and Social Psychology* 53 (3): 497.

Dietrich, Arne. 2004. "The Cognitive Neuroscience of Creativity." *Psychonomic Bulletin & Review* 11 (6): 1011–26. https://doi.org/10.3758/BF03196731.

Dixon-Román, Ezekiel. 2017. *Inheriting Possibility: Social Reproduction and Quantification in Education*. Minneapolis: University of Minnesota Press.

Dohmatob, Elvis, Yunzhen Feng, and Julia Kempe. 2024. "Model Collapse Demystified: The Case of Regression." *arXiv Preprint arXiv:2402.07712*.

Dohmatob, Elvis, Yunzhen Feng, Pu Yang, Francois Charton, and Julia Kempe. 2024. "A Tale of Tails: Model Collapse as a Change of Scaling Laws." *arXiv Preprint arXiv:2402.07043*.

Domingos, Pedro. 2000. "Bayesian Averaging of Classifiers and the Overfitting Problem." In *ICML (International Conference on Machine Learning)* (747): 223–30.

Dupré, John. 1993. *The Disorder of Things: Metaphysical Foundations of the Disunity of Science*. Cambridge, MA: Harvard University Press.

Jingfang, Hao. 2017. "Education Must Foster Creativity – and Fight Inequality." World Economic Forum, June 26, 2017. www.weforum.org/agenda/2017/06/teaching-creativity-is-key-to-reducing-inequality-here-s-why/.

Eitam, Baruch, Ran R. Hassin, and Yaacov Schul. 2008. "Nonconscious Goal Pursuit in Novel Environments: The Case of Implicit Learning." *Psychological Science* 19 (3): 261–67.

Engell, James. 1981. *The Creative Imagination: Enlightenment to Romanticism*. Cambridge, MA: Harvard University Press.

Eppe, Manfred, Ewen Maclean, Roberto Confalonieri, et al. 2018. "A Computational Framework for Conceptual Blending." *Artificial Intelligence* 256 (March): 105–29. https://doi.org/10.1016/j.artint.2017.11.005.

Epstude, Kai, and Neal J. Roese. 2007. "Beyond Rationality: Counterfactual Thinking and Behavior Regulation." *Behavioral and Brain Sciences* 30 (5–6): 457–58. https://doi.org/10.1017/S0140525X07002634.

2011. "When Goal Pursuit Fails: The Functions of Counterfactual Thought in Intention Formation." *Social Psychology* 42 (1): 19–27. https://doi.org/10.1027/1864-9335/a000039.

Epstude, Kai, Annika Scholl, and Neal J. Roese. 2016. "Prefactual Thoughts: Mental Simulations about What Might Happen." *Review of General Psychology* 20 (1): 48–56. https://doi.org/10.1037/gpr0000064.

Fabry, Regina E., and Karin Kukkonen. 2019. "Reconsidering the Mind-Wandering Reader: Predictive Processing, Probability Designs, and Enculturation." *Frontiers in Psychology* 9: 409593. www.frontiersin.org/articles/10.3389/fpsyg.2018.02648.

Fedyk, Mark, and Fei Xu. 2021. "Creativity as Potentially Valuable Improbable Constructions." *European Journal for Philosophy of Science* 11 (1): 27. https://doi.org/10.1007/s13194-020-00343-4.

Fernández-Loría, Carlos, Foster Provost, and Xintian Han. 2020. "Explaining Data-Driven Decisions Made by AI Systems: The Counterfactual Approach." *arXiv preprint arXiv:2001.07417*.

Fletcher, Angus. 2021a. "Why Computers Will Never Read (or Write) Literature: A Logical Proof and a Narrative." *Narrative* 29: 1–28.

2021b. *Wonderworks*. New York: Simon & Schuster.

2022a. "3 Exercises to Boost Your Team's Creativity." *Harvard Business Review*, March 24, 2022. https://hbr.org/2022/03/3-exercises-to-boost-your-teams-creativity.

2022b. *Creative Thinking: A Field Guide to Strengthening Your Creative Core*. US Army Command and General Staff College.

2022c. "Why Computer AI Will Never Do What We Imagine It Can." *Narrative* 30: 114–37.

2023. *Storythinking: The New Science of Narrative Intelligence*. New York: Columbia University Press.

2024a. "A New Science of Aesthetics: The Dual Brain Mechanics of Wonder, Beauty, and the Sublime." In *Routledge Companion to Literature and Art*, edited by Cheryl Julia Lee, Neil Murphy, and W. Michelle Wang, 72–83. New York: Routledge.

2024b. "Shakespeare Didn't Brainstorm: Why Literature Proves that There's More to Intelligence than AI." In *Routledge Companion to Literature and Artificial Intelligence*, edited by Genevieve Lively, and Will Slocombe, 72–83. New York: Routledge.

2025. *Primal Intelligence*. New York: Penguin Random House.

Fletcher, Angus, and Mike Benveniste. 2022. "A New Method for Training Creativity: Narrative as an Alternative to Divergent Thinking." *Annals of the New York Academy of Sciences* 1512 (1): 29–45. https://doi.org/10.1111/nyas.14763.

Fletcher, Angus, Patricia Enciso, and Mike Benveniste. 2023. "Narrative Creativity Training: A New Method for Increasing Resilience in Elementary Students." *Journal of Creativity* 33 (3): 100061. https://doi.org/10.1016/j.yjoc.2023.100061.

Fletcher, Angus, Thomas L. Gaines, and Brittany Loney. 2023. "How to Be a Better Leader Amid Volatility, Uncertainty, Complexity, and Ambiguity." *Harvard Business Review*, 28 September.

Florida, Richard. 2006. "The Flight of the Creative Class: The New Global Competition for Talent." *Liberal Education* 92 (3): 22–29.

2019. *The Rise of the Creative Class*. New York: Basic books.

Fox, Kieran C.R., and Roger E. Beaty. 2019. "Mind-Wandering as Creative Thinking: Neural, Psychological, and Theoretical Considerations." *Current Opinion in Behavioral Sciences, Creativity* (27): 123–30. https://doi.org/10.1016/j.cobeha.2018.10.009.

Franceschelli, Giorgio, and Mirco Musolesi. 2024. "Creativity and Machine Learning: A Survey." *ACM Computing Surveys*, 56 (11): 1–41. https://doi.org/10.1145/3664595.

Frensch, Peter A., and Robert J. Sternberg. 2014. "Expertise and Intelligent Thinking: When Is It Worse to Know Better?" In *Advances in the Psychology of Human Intelligence*, Vol. 5, edited by Robert J. Sternberg, 157–88. New York: Psychology Press.

Fu, Zhongzheng, Daw-An J. Wu, Ian Ross, et al. 2019. "Single-Neuron Correlates of Error Monitoring and Post-Error Adjustments in Human Medial Frontal Cortex." *Neuron* 101 (1): 165–77.

Fukushima, Kunihiko. 1988. "A Neural Network for Visual Pattern Recognition." *Computer* 21 (3): 65–75.

Furnham, Adrian. 2000. "The Brainstorming Myth." *Business Strategy Review* 11 (4): 21–28. https://doi.org/10.1111/1467-8616.00154.

Gaessler, Fabian, and Henning Piezunka. 2023. "Training with AI: Evidence from Chess Computers." *Strategic Management Journal* 44 (11): 2724–50. https://doi.org/10.1002/smj.3512.

Galilei, Galileo. 1953. *A Dialogue Concerning Two World Systems*. Edited by Stillman Drake. Oakland, CA: University of California Press.

Gao, Jinglong, Xiao Ding, Bing Qin, and Ting Liu. 2023. "Is Chatgpt a Good Causal Reasoner? A Comprehensive Evaluation." *arXiv Preprint arXiv:2305.07375*.

García, Emma. 2014. "The Need to Address Non-cognitive Skills in the Education Policy Agenda." *EPI Briefing Paper* 386. Washington, DC: Economic Policy Institute. https://doi.org/10.1007/978-94-6300-591-3_3.

Garrison, Mark J. 2009. *A Measure of Failure: The Political Origins of Standardized Testing*. State University of New York Press.

Gawdat, Mo. 2022. *Scary Smart: The Future of Artificial Intelligence and How You Can Save Our World*. London: Pan Macmillan.

Genco, Nicole, Katja Hölttä-Otto, and Carolyn Conner Seepersad. 2012. "An Experimental Investigation of the Innovation Capabilities of Undergraduate Engineering Students." *Journal of Engineering Education* 101 (1): 60–81. https://doi.org/10.1002/j.2168-9830.2012.tb00041.x.

Glăveanu, Vlad Petre. 2011. "Children and Creativity: A Most (Un)Likely Pair?" *Thinking Skills and Creativity* 6 (2): 122–31. https://doi.org/10.1016/j.tsc.2011.03.002.

2015. "Creativity as a Sociocultural Act." *The Journal of Creative Behavior* 49 (3): 165–80. https://doi.org/10.1002/jocb.94.

2020. "A Sociocultural Theory of Creativity: Bridging the Social, the Material, and the Psychological." *Review of General Psychology* 24 (4): 335–54. https://doi.org/10.1177/1089268020961763.

Glymour, Clark, Kun Zhang, and Peter Spirtes. 2019. "Review of Causal Discovery Methods Based on Graphical Models." *Frontiers in Genetics* 10: 524.

Goddu, Mariel K., and Alison Gopnik. 2020. "Learning What to Change: Young Children Use 'Difference-Making' to Identify Causally Relevant Variables." *Developmental Psychology* 56 (2): 275–84. https://doi.org/10.1037/dev0000872.

————. 2024. "The Development of Human Causal Learning and Reasoning." *Nature Reviews Psychology* (3): 319–339. https://doi.org/10.1038/s44159-024-00300-5

Goddu, Mariel K., Tania Lombrozo, and Alison Gopnik. 2020. "Transformations and Transfer: Preschool Children Understand Abstract Relations and Reason Analogically in a Causal Task." *Child Development* 91 (6): 1898–915. https://doi.org/10.1111/cdev.13412.

Goddu, Mariel K., J. Nicholas Sullivan, and Caren M. Walker. 2021. "Toddlers Learn and Flexibly Apply Multiple Possibilities." *Child Development* 92 (6): 2244–51. https://doi.org/10.1111/cdev.13668.

Gonthier, Corentin, and Maud Besançon. 2022. "It Is Not Always Better to Have More Ideas: Serial Order and the Trade-Off between Fluency and Elaboration in Divergent Thinking Tasks." *Psychology of Aesthetics, Creativity, and the Arts*, Advance online publication. https://doi-org.proxy.lib.ohio-state.edu/10.1037/aca0000485.

Goodman, Nelson. 1983. *Fact, Fiction, and Forecast*. Cambridge, MA: Harvard University Press.

Gopnik, Alison, Daphna Buchsbaum, and Elizabeth Seiver. 2013. "How Causal Learning Helps Us Understand Other People and How Other People Help Us Learn about Causes." In *Navigating the Social World*, edited by Mahzarin R. Banaji, and Susan A. Gelman, 186–90. Oxford, UK: Oxford University Press. https://doi.org/10.1093/acprof:oso/9780199890712.003.0034.

Gopnik, Alison, Clark Glymour, David M. Sobel, et al. 2004. "A Theory of Causal Learning in Children: Causal Maps and Bayes Nets." *Psychological Review* 111 (1): 3–32. https://doi.org/10.1037/0033-295X.111.1.3.

Gopnik, Alison, and Laura Schulz, eds. 2007. *Causal Learning: Psychology, Philosophy, and Computation*. Oxford: Oxford University Press.

Gopnik, Alison, David M. Sobel, Laura E. Schulz, and Clark Glymour. 2001. "Causal Learning Mechanisms in Very Young Children: Two-, Three-, and Four-Year-Olds Infer Causal Relations from Patterns of Variation and Covariation." *Developmental Psychology* 37 (5): 620–29. https://doi.org/10.1037/0012-1649.37.5.620.

Gopnik, Alison, and Caren M. Walker. 2013. "Considering Counterfactuals: The Relationship between Causal Learning and Pretend Play." *American Journal of Play* 6 (1): 15–28.

Gottlieb, Derek. 2020. *A Democratic Theory of Educational Accountability: From Test-Based Assessment to Interpersonal Responsibility.* New York: Routledge. https://doi.org/10.4324/9780429019159.

Grant, Adam M., and James W. Berry. 2011. "The Necessity of Others Is the Mother of Invention: Intrinsic and Prosocial Motivations, Perspective Taking, and Creativity." *Academy of Management Journal* 54 (1): 73–96. https://doi.org/10.5465/amj.2011.59215085.

Greenblatt, Stephen. 2012. *The Swerve: How the World Became Modern.* New York: Norton.

Gu, Xiaojing, Simone M. Ritter, Lea R. Delfmann, and Ap Dijksterhuis. 2022. "Stimulating Creativity: Examining the Effectiveness of Four Cognitive-Based Creativity Training Techniques." *The Journal of Creative Behavior* 56 (3): 312–27. https://doi.org/10.1002/jocb.531.

Gualtieri, Samantha, and Amy S. Finn. 2022. "The Sweet Spot: When Children's Developing Abilities, Brains, and Knowledge Make Them Better Learners than Adults." *Perspectives on Psychological Science* 17 (5): 1322–38. https://doi.org/10.1177/17456916211045971.

Guilford, Joy Paul. 1950. "Creativity." *American Psychologist* 5 (9): 444–54. https://doi.org/10.1037/h0063487.

1956. "The Structure of Intellect." *Psychological Bulletin* 53 (4): 267–93. https://doi.org/10.1037/h0040755.

1967. "Creativity: Yesterday, Today and Tomorrow." *The Journal of Creative Behavior* 1 (1): 3–14. https://doi.org/10.1002/j.2162-6057.1967.tb00002.x.

1968. *Intelligence, Creativity, and Their Educational Implications.* San Diego, CA: R. R. Knapp.

Hammell, Cecilia, and Amy Y. C. Chan. 2016. "Improving Physical Task Performance with Counterfactual and Prefactual Thinking." *PLOS ONE* 11 (12): e0168181. https://doi.org/10.1371/journal.pone.0168181.

Harré, Rom, and Edward H. Madden. 1975. *Causal Powers: A Theory of Natural Necessity.* Totowa, NJ: Rowman and Littlefield.

Harris, Phillip, Bruce M. Smith, and Joan Harris. 2011. *The Myths of Standardized Tests: Why They Don't Tell You What You Think They Do.* Lanham, MD: Rowman & Littlefield.

Hass, Richard W. 2017a. "Semantic Search during Divergent Thinking." *Cognition* 166 (September): 344–57. https://doi.org/10.1016/j.cognition.2017.05.039.

2017b. "Tracking the Dynamics of Divergent Thinking via Semantic Distance: Analytic Methods and Theoretical Implications." *Memory & Cognition* 45 (2): 233–44. https://doi.org/10.3758/s13421-016-0659-y.

Hassabis, Demis. 2017. "Artificial Intelligence: Chess Match of the Century." *Nature* 544: 413–14.

Hassin, Ran R., Henk Aarts, Baruch Eitam, Ruud Custers, and Tali Kleiman. 2009. "Non-conscious Goal Pursuit and the Effortful Control of Behavior." In *Oxford Handbook of Human Action*, edited by Ezequiel Morsella, John A. Bargh, and Peter M. Gollwitzer, 549–66. Oxford, UK: Oxford University Press.

Hawkins, Douglas M. 2004. "The Problem of Overfitting." *Journal of Chemical Information and Computer Sciences* 44 (1): 1–12.

He, Yuejun, Bradley Camburn, Haowen Liu, et al. 2019. "Mining and Representing the Concept Space of Existing Ideas for Directed Ideation." *Journal of Mechanical Design* 141 (12): 121101. https://doi.org/10.1115/1.4044399.

Henriksen, Danah, Edwin Creely, and Michael Henderson. 2019. "Failing in Creativity: The Problem of Policy and Practice in Australia and the United States." *Kappa Delta Pi Record* 55 (1): 4–10. https://doi.org/10.1080/00228958.2019.1549429.

Herman, David. 2009. "Cognitive Narratology." In *The Handbook of Narratology*, edited by Peter Hühn, Jan Christoph Meister, John Pier and Wolf Schmid, 30–43. *Narratologia: Contributions to Narrative Theory* 19. Berlin, GE: De Gruyter.

2017. *Storytelling and the Sciences of Mind*. Cambridge, MA: MIT Press.

Houdé, Olivier, and Nathalie Tzourio-Mazoyer. 2003. "Neural Foundations of Logical and Mathematical Cognition." *Nature Reviews Neuroscience* 4: 507–14.

Huang, Biwei, Kun Zhang, Jiji Zhang, et al. 2020. "Causal Discovery from Heterogeneous/Nonstationary Data." *Journal of Machine Learning Research* 21 (89): 1–53.

Hubert, Kent F., Kim N. Awa, and Darya L. Zabelina. 2024. "The Current State of Artificial Intelligence Generative Language Models Is More Creative than Humans on Divergent Thinking Tasks." *Scientific Reports* 14 (1): 3440. https://doi.org/10.1038/s41598-024-53303-w.

Hui, Anna N. N., Mavis W. J. He, and Wan-chi Wong. 2019. "Understanding the Development of Creativity across the Life Span." In *The Cambridge Handbook of Creativity*, edited by James C. Kaufman, and Robert J. Sternberg, 2nd ed., 69–87. Cambridge Handbooks in Psychology. Cambridge: Cambridge University Press. https://doi.org/10.1017/9781316979839.006.

Hume, David. 2007. *A Treatise of Human Nature: A Critical Edition*. Edited by David Fate Norton and Mary J. Norton. Oxford: Clarendon Press.

———. 1993. *An Enquiry Concerning Human Understanding; [with] A Letter from a Gentleman to His Friend in Edinburgh; [and] An Abstract of a Treatise of Human Nature*. Edited by Eric Steinberg. Indianapolis, IN: Hackett.

Husain, Amir. 2017. *The Sentient Machine: The Coming Age of Artificial Intelligence*. New York: Simon and Schuster.

Huxley, Julian S. 2009. *Evolution: The Modern Synthesis, the Definitive Edition*. Edited by Massimo Pigliucci, and Gerd B. Müller. Cambridge, MA: MIT Press.

Imanaka, Kuniyasu, Ichiro Kita, and Kunitake Suzuki. 2002. "Effects of Non conscious Perception on Motor Response." *Human Movement Science* 21 (5–6): 541–61.

Jin, Zhijing, Jiarui Liu, Zhiheng Lyu, et al. 2023. "Can Large Language Models Infer Causation from Correlation?" *arXiv Preprint arXiv:2306.05836*.

Jing, Delin, and Hongji Yang. 2015. "Creative Computing for Bespoke Ideation." In *2015 IEEE 39th Annual Computer Software and Applications Conference*, 34–43. Taichung, Taiwan: IEEE. https://doi.org/10.1109/COMPSAC .2015.203.

Johnson-Laird, Philip Nicholas, and Sangeet Khemlani. 2017. "Mental Models and Causation." In *Oxford Handbook of Causal Reasoning*, edited by Michael R. Waldmann, 1–42. New York: Oxford University Press .

Kaas, Jon H. 2020. "Evolution of Visual Cortex in Primates." In *Evolutionary Neuroscience*, edited by Jon H. Kaas, 2nd ed., 547–64. Netherlands: Academic Press.

Kahneman, Daniel. 1995. "Varieties of Counterfactual Thinking." In *What Might Have Been: The Social Psychology of Counterfactual Thinking*, edited by Neal J. Roese and James M. Olson, 375–96. Hillsdale, NJ: Lawrence Erlbaum Associates.

———. 2011. *Thinking, Fast and Slow*. New York: Farrar, Straus and Giroux.

Kahneman, Daniel, and Dale T. Miller. 1986. "Norm Theory: Comparing Reality to Its Alternatives." *Psychological Review* 93 (2): 136.

Kalargiros, Emmanuel M., and Michael R. Manning. 2015. "Divergent Thinking and Brainstorming in Perspective: Implications for Organization Change and Innovation." In *Research in Organizational Change and Development*, edited by Abraham B. (Rami) Shani and Debra A. Noumair, 23: 293–327. Emerald Group Publishing Limited. https://doi.org/10.1108/S0897-301620150000023007.

Kaufman, James C., John Baer, and Jason C. Cole. 2009. "Expertise, Domains, and the Consensual Assessment Technique." *The Journal of Creative*

Behavior 43 (4): 223–33. https://doi.org/10.1002/j.2162-6057.2009 .tb01316.x.

Kaufman, James C., John Baer, Jason C. Cole, and Janel D. Sexton. 2008. "A Comparison of Expert and Nonexpert Raters Using the Consensual Assessment Technique." *Creativity Research Journal* 20 (2): 171–78. https://doi.org/10.1080/10400410802059929.

Kaufman, James C., Joohyun Lee, John Baer, and Soonmook Lee. 2007. "Captions, Consistency, Creativity, and the Consensual Assessment Technique: New Evidence of Reliability." *Thinking Skills and Creativity* 2 (2): 96–106. https://doi.org/10.1016/j.tsc.2007.04.002.

Keenan-Lechel, Sarah F., Danah Henriksen, and the Deep-Play Research Group. 2019. "Creativity as Perspective Taking: An Interview with Dr. Vlad Glăveanu." *TechTrends* 63 (6): 652–58. https://doi.org/10.1007/ s11528-019-00437-8.

Keijzer, Fred, Mark Duijn, and Pamela Lyon. 2013. "What Nervous Systems Do: Early Evolution, Input-Output, and the Skin Brain Thesis." *Adaptive Behaviour* 21: 67–85.

Kempf, Arlo. 2016. *The Pedagogy of Standardized Testing: The Radical Impacts of Educational Standardization in the US and Canada*. New York: Palgrave Macmillan.

Kenett, Yoed N. 2018. "Going the Extra Creative Mile: The Role of Semantic Distance in Creativity – Theory, Research, and Measurement." *The Cambridge Handbook of the Neuroscience of Creativity* 3: 233–48.

2019. "What Can Quantitative Measures of Semantic Distance Tell Us about Creativity?" *Current Opinion in Behavioral Sciences*, Creativity, 27 (June): 11–16. https://doi.org/10.1016/j.cobeha.2018.08.010.

Kenett, Yoed N., Effi Levi, David Anaki, and Miriam Faust. 2017. "The Semantic Distance Task: Quantifying Semantic Distance with Semantic Network Path Length." *Journal of Experimental Psychology: Learning, Memory, and Cognition* 43 (9): 1470–89. https://doi.org/10.1037/xlm0000391.

Kıcıman, Emre, Robert Ness, Amit Sharma, and Chenhao Tan. 2023. "Causal Reasoning and Large Language Models: Opening a New Frontier for Causality." *arXiv Preprint arXiv:2305.00050*.

Kim, Kyung Hee. 2011. "The Creativity Crisis: The Decrease in Creative Thinking Scores on the Torrance Tests of Creative Thinking." *Creativity Research Journal* 23 (4): 285–95. https://doi.org/10.1080/10400419.2011.627805.

2016. *The Creativity Challenge: How We Can Recapture American Innovation*. Amherst, NY: Prometheus Books.

Knauff, Markus. 2007. "How Our Brains Reason Logically." *Topoi-An International Review of Philosophy* 26 (1): 19–36.

Kolko, Jon. 2014. *Well-Designed: How to Use Empathy to Create Products People Love*. Boston, MA: Harvard Business Review Press.

Koretz, Daniel. 2017. *The Testing Charade: Pretending to Make Schools Better*. University of Chicago Press. https://doi.org/10.7208/chicago/9780226408859.001.0001.

Koskinen, Ilpo. 2023. *Design, Empathy, Interpretation: Toward Interpretive Design Research*. Design Thinking, Design Theory. Cambridge, MA: The MIT Press.

Kosoy, Eliza, David M. Chan, Adrian Liu, et al. 2022. "Towards Understanding How Machines Can Learn Causal Overhypotheses." *arXiv preprint arXiv:2206.08353*.

Kristan, William B. 2016. "Early Evolution of Neurons." *Current Biology* 26 (20): R949–R954. https://doi.org/10.1016/j.cub.2016.05.030.

Kukkonen, Karin. 2020. *Probability Designs: Literature and Predictive Processing*. Oxford, UK: Oxford University Press.

Kupers, Ron, Pietro Pietrini, Emiliano Ricciardi, and Maurice Ptito. 2011. "The Nature of Consciousness in the Visually Deprived Brain." *Frontiers in Psychology* 2: 19.

Kurzweil, Ray. 2000. *The Age of Spiritual Machines: When Computers Exceed Human Intelligence*. New York: Penguin.

Lagnado, David A., and Steven Sloman. 2019. "Learning Causal Structure." In *Proceedings of the Twenty-Fourth Annual Conference of the Cognitive Science Society*, edited by Wayne D. Gray, and Christian D. Schunn, 1st ed., 560–65. London: Routledge. https://doi.org/10.4324/9781315782379-132.

Land, George, and Beth Jarman. 1993. *Breakpoint and Beyond: Mastering the Future Today*. New York: Harper Business.

Larson, Erik J. 2021. *The Myth of Artificial Intelligence*. Cambridge, MA: Harvard University Press.

Lavrič, Franc, and Andrej Škraba. 2023. "Brainstorming Will Never Be the Same Again – A Human Group Supported by Artificial Intelligence." *Machine Learning and Knowledge Extraction* 5 (4): 1282–301. https://doi.org/10.3390/make5040065.

Lee, Alexis W., and Sandra W. Russ. 2021. "Development of Creativity in School-Age Children." In *The Cambridge Handbook of Lifespan Development of Creativity*, edited by Sandra W. Russ, Jessica D. Hoffmann, and James C. Kaufman, 1st ed., 126–38. Cambridge, UK: Cambridge University Press. https://doi.org/10.1017/9781108755726.009.

Lee, Sam Youl, Richard Florida, and Gary Gates. 2010. "Innovation, Human Capital, and Creativity." *International Review of Public Administration* 14 (3): 13–24. https://doi.org/10.1080/12294659.2010.10805158.

Legare, Cristine H., David M. Sobel, and Maureen Callanan. 2017. "Causal Learning Is Collaborative: Examining Explanation and Exploration in Social Contexts." *Psychonomic Bulletin & Review* 24 (5): 1548–54. https://doi.org/10.3758/s13423-017-1351-3.

Lemann, Nicholas. 2024. *Higher Admissions: The Rise and Fall of Standardized Testing*. Princeton, NJ: Princeton University Press.

Leo, Mengyu, Jiaojioao Li, Simonida Subotić, and Lena Woodward (World Economic Forum Project Team). 2015. "'The Skills Needed in the 21st Century – New Vision for Education' from New Vision for Education: Fostering Social and Emotional Learning through Technology," In *New Vision for Education: Unlocking the Potential of Technology*. Geneva: World Economic Forum. https://widgets.weforum.org/nve-2015/index.html

Levesque, Hector J. 2018. *Common Sense, the Turing Test, and the Quest for Real AI*. Cambridge, MA: MIT Press.

Lewis, David. 1973. *Counterfactuals*. Cambridge, MA: Harvard University Press.

1979. "Counterfactual Dependence and Time's Arrow." *Noûs*, (13): 455–76.

Lewrick, Michael, Patrick Link, and Larry Leifer. 2018. *The Design Thinking Playbook: Mindful Digital Transformation of Teams, Products, Services, Businesses and Ecosystems*. Hoboken, NJ: Wiley.

Licuanan, B. F., L. R. Dailey, and M. D. Mumford. 2007. "Idea Evaluation: Error in Evaluating Highly Original Ideas." *The Journal of Creative Behavior* 41: 1–27.

Liebeskind, Benjamin J., David M. Hillis, Harold H. Zakon, and Hans A. Hofmann. 2016. "Complex Homology and the Evolution of Nervous Systems." *Trends in Ecology & Evolution* 31 (2): 127–35.

Liebeskind, Benjamin J., Hans A. Hofmann, David M. Hillis, and Harold H. Zakon. 2017. "Evolution of Animal Neural Systems." *Annual Review of Ecology, Evolution, and Systematics* 48: 377–98.

Liquin, Emily G., and Alison Gopnik. 2022. "Children Are More Exploratory and Learn More than Adults in an Approach-Avoid Task." *Cognition* 218 (January): 104940. https://doi.org/10.1016/j.cognition.2021.104940.

Liquin, Emily G., and Tania Lombrozo. 2020a. "A Functional Approach to Explanation-Seeking Curiosity." *Cognitive Psychology* 119 (June): 101276.

2020b. "Explanation-Seeking Curiosity in Childhood." *Current Opinion in Behavioral Sciences* 35 (October): 14–20. https://doi.org/10.1016/j.cobeha.2020.05.012.

Liu, Xiaoyu, Paiheng Xu, Junda Wu, et al. 2024. "Large Language Models and Causal Inference in Collaboration: A Comprehensive Survey." *arXiv Preprint arXiv:2403.09606*.

Lombrozo, Tania. 2012. "Explanation and Abductive Inference." In *The Oxford Handbook of Thinking and Reasoning*, 260–76. Oxford Library of Psychology. New York: Oxford University Press.

Lopata, Joel A., Nathaniel Barr, Matthew Slayton, and Paul Seli. 2022. "Dual-Modes of Creative Thought in the Classroom: Implications of Network Neuroscience for Creativity Education." *Translational Issues in Psychological Science*, 8 (1): 79–89. https://doi.org/10.1037/tps0000317.

Lu, Hongjing, Nicholas Ichien, and Keith J. Holyoak. 2022. "Probabilistic Analogical Mapping with Semantic Relation Networks." *Psychological Review* 129 (5): 1078–103. https://doi.org/10.1037/rev0000358.

Lucas, Christopher G., Sophie Bridgers, Thomas L. Griffiths, and Alison Gopnik. 2014. "When Children Are Better (or at Least More Open-Minded) Learners than Adults: Developmental Differences in Learning the Forms of Causal Relationships." *Cognition* 131 (2): 284–99. https://doi.org/10.1016/j.cognition.2013.12.010.

Ma, Xiaoya, Xianguang Hou, Gregory D. Edgecombe, and Nicholas J. Strausfeld. 2012. "Complex Brain and Optic Lobes in an Early Cambrian Arthropod." *Nature* 490 (7419): 258–61.

Mackie, John Leslie. 1980. *The Cement of the Universe: A Study of Causation*. Oxford, UK: Clarendon Press.

Magnani, Lorenzo. 2009. *Abductive Cognition: The Epistemological and Eco-Cognitive Dimensions of Hypothetical Reasoning*. Vol. 3. *Cognitive Systems Monographs*. Berlin: Springer. https://doi.org/10.1007/978-3-642-03631-6.

——— 2017. "Not Everything in Scientific Cognition Is Evidence-Based." In *The Abductive Structure of Scientific Creativity: An Essay on the Ecology of Cognition*, edited by Lorenzo Magnani, 47–64. Studies in Applied Philosophy, Epistemology and Rational Ethics. Cham: Springer International. https://doi.org/10.1007/978-3-319-59256-5_3.

Magnani, Lorenzo, Walter Carnielli, and Claudio Pizzi, eds. 2010. *Model-Based Reasoning in Science and Technology: Abduction, Logic, and Computational Discovery*. Vol. 314. Studies in Computational Intelligence. Berlin: Springer. https://doi.org/10.1007/978-3-642-15223-8.

Mandel, David R. 2003. "Effect of Counterfactual and Factual Thinking on Causal Judgements." *Thinking & Reasoning* 9 (3): 245–65. https://doi.org/10.1080/13546780343000231.

Marron, Tali R., Yulia Lerner, Ety Berant, et al. 2018. "Chain Free Association, Creativity, and the Default Mode Network." *Neuropsychologia* 118 (September): 40–58. https://doi.org/10.1016/j.neuropsychologia.2018.03.018.

Mateja, Deborah, and Armin Heinzl. 2021. "Towards Machine Learning as an Enabler of Computational Creativity." *IEEE Transactions on Artificial Intelligence* 2 (6): 460–75. https://doi.org/10.1109/TAI.2021.3100456.

Mayr, Ernst. 1993. "What Was the Evolutionary Synthesis?" *Trends in Ecology and Evolution* 8: 31–34.

McCormack, Teresa, Victoria Simms, Jemma McGourty, and Tom Beckers. 2013. "Encouraging Children to Think Counterfactually Enhances Blocking in a Causal Learning Task." *Quarterly Journal of Experimental Psychology* 66 (10): 1910–26. https://doi.org/10.1080/17470218.2013.767847.

McEleney, Alice, and Ruth M. J. Byrne. 2006. "Spontaneous Counterfactual Thoughts and Causal Explanations." *Thinking & Reasoning* 12 (2): 235–55. https://doi.org/10.1080/13546780500317897.

Mednick, Sarnoff. 1962. "The Associative Basis of the Creative Process." *Psychological Review* 69 (3): 220–32. https://doi.org/10.1037/h0048850.

Mekern, Vera, Bernhard Hommel, and Zsuzsika Sjoerds. 2019. "Computational Models of Creativity: A Review of Single-Process and Multi-Process Recent Approaches to Demystify Creative Cognition." *Current Opinion in Behavioral Sciences* 27 (June): 47–54. https://doi.org/10.1016/j.cobeha.2018.09.008.

Mekern, Vera N., Zsuzsika Sjoerds, and Bernhard Hommel. 2019. "How Metacontrol Biases and Adaptivity Impact Performance in Cognitive Search Tasks." *Cognition* 182 (January): 251–59. https://doi.org/10.1016/j.cognition.2018.10.001.

Mercier, Hugo, and Dan Sperber. 2017. *The Enigma of Reason.* Cambridge, MA: Harvard University Press.

Michael, William B. 1999. "Guilford's View." In *Encyclopedia of Creativity*, Vol. 1, edited by Mark Runco, and Steven Pitzker, 785–97. San Diego, CA: Academic Press.

Michotte, A. 2017. *The Perception of Causality.* Psychology Library Editions: Perception. Albert Michotte Milton Park, UK: Taylor & Francis.

Millar, Susanna. 1968. *The Psychology of Play.* London: Penguin.

Minai, Ali A., Simona Doboli, and Laxmi R. Iyer. 2021. "Models of Creativity and Ideation: An Overview." In *Creativity and Innovation: Cognitive, Social, and Computational Approaches*, edited by Simona Doboli, Jared B. Kenworthy, Ali A. Minai, and Paul B. Paulus, 21–45. Cham, Switzerland: Springer. https://doi.org/10.1007/978-3-030-77198-0_2.

Misra, Shashank, Leslie C. Bland, Suma G. Cardwell, et al. 2023. "Probabilistic Neural Computing with Stochastic Devices." *Advanced Materials* 35 (37): 2204569. https://doi.org/10.1002/adma.202204569.

Monk, Travis, and Michael G. Paulin. 2014. "Predation and the Origin of Neurons." *Brain Behavior Evolution* 84: 246–61.

Monti, Martin M., and Daniel N. Osherson. 2012. "Logic, Language and the Brain." *Brain Research* 1428 (January): 33–42.

Mooij, Joris M., Dominik Janzing, and Bernhard Schölkopf. 2013. "From Ordinary Differential Equations to Structural Causal Models: The Deterministic Case." *arXiv Preprint arXiv:1304.7920.*

Moroz, Leonid L., and Daria Y. Romanova. 2022. "Alternative Neural Systems: What Is a Neuron? (Ctenophores, sponges and placozoans)." *Frontiers in Cell and Developmental Biology* 10: 1071961. https://doi.org/10.3389/fcell.2022.1071961.

Moroz, Leonid L., and Andrea B. Kohn. 2016. "Independent Origins of Neurons and Synapses: Insights from Ctenophores." *Philosophical Transactions of the Royal Society of London B* 371: 1–14.

Mullen, Brian, Craig Johnson, and Eduardo Salas. 1991. "Productivity Loss in Brainstorming Groups: A Meta-Analytic Integration." *Basic and Applied Social Psychology* 12 (1): 3–23. https://doi.org/10.1207/s15324834 basp1201_1.

Muller, Jerry Z. 2019. *The Tyranny of Metrics*. Princeton, NJ: Princeton University Press.

Mumford, Michael D. 2001. "Something Old, Something New: Revisiting Guilford's Conception of Creative Problem Solving." *Creativity Research Journal* 13 (3–4): 267–76. https://doi.org/10.1207/S15326934CRJ1334_04.

Mumford, Michael D., Cassie Blair, Lesley Dailey, Lyle E. Leritz, and Holly K. Osburn. 2006. "Errors in Creative Thought? Cognitive Biases in a Complex Processing Activity." *The Journal of Creative Behavior* 40 (2): 75–109. https://doi.org/10.1002/j.2162-6057.2006.tb01267.x.

Mumford, Michael D., and Robert W. Martin. 2020. "Analogies." In *Encyclopedia of Creativity*, edited by Steven Pritzker, and Mark Runco, 3rd ed., 37–41. Oxford: Academic Press. https://doi.org/10.1016/B978-0-12-809324-5.23692-4.

Mumford, Michael D., and Tristan McIntosh. 2017. "Creative Thinking Processes: The Past and the Future." *The Journal of Creative Behavior* 51 (4): 317–22. https://doi.org/10.1002/jocb.197.

Nahin, Paul. 2017. *The Logician and the Engineer: How George Boole and Claude Shannon Created the Information Age*. Princeton, NJ: Princeton University Press.

Naveed, Humza, Asad Ullah Khan, Shi Qiu, et al. 2023. "A Comprehensive Overview of Large Language Models." *arXiv Preprint arXiv:2307.06435.*

Nersessian, Nancy J. 2008. *Creating Scientific Concepts*. Cambridge, MA: MIT Press.

Ney, Steven, and Christoph Meinel. 2019. *Putting Design Thinking to Work: How Large Organizations Can Embrace Messy Institutions to Tackle Wicked Problems*. Cham: Springer International. https://doi.org/10.1007/978-3-030-19609-7.

Nickles, Thomas. 1994. "Enlightenment versus Romantic Models of Creativity in Science – and Beyond." *Creativity Research Journal* 7 (3–4): 277–314. https://doi.org/10.1080/10400419409534535.

Nogueira, Ana Rita, Andrea Pugnana, Salvatore Ruggieri, Dino Pedreschi, and João Gama. 2022. "Methods and Tools for Causal Discovery and Causal Inference." *Wiley Interdisciplinary Reviews: Data Mining and Knowledge Discovery* 12 (2): 1449.

Nyhout, Angela, and Patricia A. Ganea. 2019a. "Mature Counterfactual Reasoning in 4- and 5-Year-Olds." *Cognition* 183 (February): 57–66. https://doi.org/10.1016/j.cognition.2018.10.027.

2019b. "The Development of the Counterfactual Imagination." *Child Development Perspectives* 13 (4): 254–59. https://doi.org/10.1111/cdep.12348.

2020. "What Is and What Never Should Have Been: Children's Causal and Counterfactual Judgments about the Same Events." *Journal of Experimental Child Psychology* 192 (April): 104773. https://doi.org/10.1016/j.jecp.2019.104773.

O'Brien, Frank. 2010. *The Apollo Guidance Computer: Architecture and Operation*. Berlin: Springer Science & Business Media.

O'Regan, J. Kevin, and Alva Noë. 2001. "A Sensorimotor Account of Vision and Visual Consciousness." *Behavioral and Brain Sciences* 24 (5): 939–73. https://doi.org/10.1017/S0140525X01000115.

Ortega-Hernández, Javier, Rudy Lerosey-Aubril, and Stephen Pates. 2019. "Proclivity of Nervous System Preservation in Cambrian Burgess Shale-Type Deposits." *Proceedings of the Royal Society B* 286: 20192370.

Orwig, William, Ibai Diez, Patrizia Vannini, Roger Beaty, and Jorge Sepulcre. 2021. "Creative Connections: Computational Semantic Distance Captures Individual Creativity and Resting-State Functional Connectivity." *Journal of Cognitive Neuroscience* 33 (3): 499–509. https://doi.org/10.1162/jocn_a_01658.

Osborn, Alex. 1963. *Applied Imagination: Principles and Procedures of Creative Problem-Solving*. New York: Scribner.

2008. *Your Creative Power: How to Use Your Imagination to Brighten Life, to Get Ahead*. Lanham, MD: University Press of America.

Otis, Laura. 2015. *Rethinking Thought: Inside the Minds of Creative Scientists and Artists*. Oxford, UK: Oxford University Press.

Parikh, Natasha, Luka Ruzic, Gregory W. Stewart, R. Nathan Spreng, and Felipe De Brigard. 2018. "What If? Neural Activity Underlying Semantic and Episodic Counterfactual Thinking." *NeuroImage* 178 (September): 332–45. https://doi.org/10.1016/j.neuroimage.2018.05.053.

Paulus, Paul B., and Jared B. Kenworthy. 2019. "Effective Brainstorming." In *The Oxford Handbook of Group Creativity and Innovation*, edited by Paul B. Paulus, and Bernard A. Nijstad, 287–306. Oxford: Oxford University Press.

Pearl, Judea. 1993. "[Bayesian Analysis in Expert Systems]: Comment: Graphical Models, Causality and Intervention." *Statistical Science* 8 (3): 266–69. https://doi.org/10.1214/ss/1177010894.

2009a. "Causal Inference in Statistics: An Overview." *Statistics Surveys* (3): 96–146. https://doi.org/10.1214/09-SS057.

2009b. *Causality*. Cambridge, UK: Cambridge University Press.

2023. "Judea Pearl, AI, and Causality: What Role Do Statisticians Play?" (Interviewed by D. Mackenzie). *Amstat News (AI Special Issue)* 555: 6–9.

Pellegrino, James W., and Mararet L. Hilton, eds. 2012. *Education for Life and Work: Developing Transferable Knowledge and Skills in the 21st Century*. Washington, DC: National Academies Press. https://doi.org/10.17226/13398.

Pennequin, Valérie, Floriane Questel, Emeline Delaville, Marie Delugre, and Célia Maintenant. 2020. "Metacognition and Emotional Regulation in Children from 8 to 12 Years Old." *British Journal of Educational Psychology* 90 (S1): 1–16. https://doi.org/10.1111/bjep.12305.

Peters, Jonas, Dominik Janzing, and Bernhard Scholkopf. 2017. *Elements of Causal Inference: Foundations and Learning Algorithms*. Adaptive Computation and Machine Learning Series. Cambridge, MA: MIT Press.

Pins, Delphine, and Dominic Ffytche. 2003. "The Neural Correlates of Conscious Vision." *Cerebral Cortex* 13 (5): 461–74. https://doi.org/10.1093/cercor/13.5.461.

Plucker, Jonathan A., and Gayle T. Dow. 2017. "Attitude Change as the Precursor to Creativity Enhancement." In *Nurturing Creativity in the Classroom*, edited by Ronald A. Beghetto, and James C. Kaufman, 2nd ed., 190–211. Cambridge: Cambridge University Press. https://doi.org/10.1017/9781316212899.013.

Plucker, Jonathan A., Matthew C. Makel, and Meihua Qian. 2019. "Assessment of Creativity." In *Cambridge Handbook of Creativity*, edited by James C. Kaufman, and Robert J. Sternberg, 2nd ed., 48–73. New York: Cambridge University Press.

Putman, Vicky L., and Paul B. Paulus. 2009. "Brainstorming, Brainstorming Rules and Decision Making." *The Journal of Creative Behavior* 43 (1): 29–40. https://doi.org/10.1002/j.2162-6057.2009.tb01304.x.

Radvansky, Gabriel A., and Jeffrey M. Zacks. 2014. *Event Cognition*. Oxford, UK: Oxford University Press.

Rahnamayan, Shahryar, Hamid R. Tizhoosh, and Magdy M. A. Salama. 2008. "Opposition versus Randomness in Soft Computing Techniques." *Applied Soft Computing* 8 (2): 906–18. https://doi.org/10.1016/j.asoc.2007.07.010.

Reiter-Palmon, Roni, Boris Forthmann, and Baptiste Barbot. 2019. "Scoring Divergent Thinking Tests: A Review and Systematic Framework." *Psychology of Aesthetics Creativity and the Arts* 13 (April): 144–52. https://doi.org/10.1037/aca0000227.

Risi, Sebastian, and Mike Preuss. 2020. "From Chess and Atari to StarCraft and Beyond: How Game AI Is Driving the World of AI." *Künstl Intell* 34: 7–17. https://doi.org/10.1007/s13218-020-00647-w.

Ritter, Simone M., Xiaojing Gu, Maurice Crijns, and Peter Biekens. 2020. "Fostering Students' Creative Thinking Skills by Means of a One-Year Creativity Training Program." *PLOS ONE* 15 (3): e0229773. https://doi.org/10.1371/journal.pone.0229773.

Roese, Neal J. 1997. "Counterfactual Thinking." *Psychological Bulletin* 121 (1): 133–48. https://doi.org/10.1037/0033-2909.121.1.133.

Roese, Neal J., and Kai Epstude. 2017. "The Functional Theory of Counterfactual Thinking: New Evidence, New Challenges, New Insights." In *Advances in Experimental Social Psychology*, edited by James M. Olson, 1–79, Vol. 56. Cambridge, MA: Academic Press. https://doi.org/10.1016/bs.aesp.2017.02.001.

Roese, Neal J., and Taekyun Hur. 1997. "Affective Determinants of Counterfactual Thinking." *Social Cognition* 15 (4): 274–90. https://doi.org/10.1521/soco.1997.15.4.274.

Roese, Neal J., and James M. Olson. 1997. "Counterfactual Thinking: The Intersection of Affect and Function." In *Advances in Experimental Social Psychology*, edited by Mark P. Zanna, 29: 1–59. San Diego, CA: Academic Press. https://doi.org/10.1016/S0065-2601(08)60015-5.

Root-Bernstein, Robert, and Michele Root-Bernstein. 2004. "Artistic Scientists and Scientific Artists: The Link between Polymathy and Creativity." In *Creativity: From Potential to Realization*, edited by Robert J. Sternberg, Elena L. Grigorenko, and Jerome L. Singer, 127–51. Washington, DC: American Psychological Association. https://doi.org/10.1037/10692-008.

Rosa, Marcello G., and Leah A. Krubitzer. 1999. "The Evolution of Visual Cortex: Where Is V2?" *Trends in Neuroscience* 22 (6): 242–48.

Runco, Mark A. 2020. "Divergent Thinking." In *Encyclopedia of Creativity*, edited by Steven Pritzker, and Mark Runco, 3rd ed., 356–61. Oxford: Academic Press. https://doi.org/10.1016/B978-0-12-809324-5.23824-8.

———. 2023. *Creativity: Research, Development, and Practice*, 3rd ed. London: Academic Press, an Imprint of Elsevier.

Runco, Mark A., and Garrett J. Jaeger. 2012. "The Standard Definition of Creativity." *Creativity Research Journal* 24 (1): 92–96. https://doi.org/10.1080/10400419.2012.650092.

Rury, John L. 2023. *An Age of Accountability: How Standardized Testing Came to Dominate American Schools and Compromise Education*. New Brunswick, NJ: Rutgers University Press.

Russ, Sandra W. 2020. "Chapter 10 – Mind Wandering, Fantasy, and Pretend Play: A Natural Combination." In *Creativity and the Wandering Mind*, edited by David D. Preiss, Diego Cosmelli, and James C. Kaufman, 231–48. Explorations in Creativity Research. London: Academic Press. https://doi.org/10.1016/B978-0-12-816400-6.00010-9.

Russ, Sandra W., and Jessica D. Hoffmann. 2020. "Associative Theory." In *Encyclopedia of Creativity*, edited by Steven Pritzker, and Mark Runco, 3rd ed., 76–82. Oxford: Academic Press. https://doi.org/10.1016/B978-0-12-809324-5.23800-5.

Russ, Sandra W., and Olena Zyga. 2016. "Imaginative Play." In *Creativity and Reason in Cognitive Development*, edited by James C. Kaufman, and John Baer, 2nd ed., 52–71. Cambridge: Cambridge University Press. https://doi.org/10.1017/CBO9781139941969.004.

Russell, Bertrand. 1912. "On the Notion of Cause." *Proceedings of the Aristotelian Society* 13: 1–26.

Salmon, Wesley C. 1998. *Causality and Explanation*. Oxford, UK: Oxford University Press.

Samland, Jana. 2016. "The Role of Prescriptive Norms and Knowledge in Children's and Adults' Causal Selection." *Journal of Experimental Psychology: General* 145 (2): 125. https://doi.org/10.1037/xge0000138.

Schölkopf, Bernhard. 2022. "Causality for Machine Learning." In *Probabilistic and Causal Inference: The Works of Judea Pearl*, edited by Hector Geffner, Rina Dechter, and Joseph Y. Halpern, 765–804. New York: ACM Books.

Schölkopf, Bernhard, Francesco Locatello, Stefan Bauer, et al. 2021. "Toward Causal Representation Learning." *Proceedings of the IEEE* 109 (5): 612–34.

Schwab, Ivan R. 2018. "The Evolution of Eyes: Major Steps (The Keeler Lecture 2017)." *Eye* 32 (2): 302–13.

Scott, Ginamarie, Lyle E. Leritz, and Michael D. Mumford. 2004a. "The Effectiveness of Creativity Training: A Quantitative Review." *Creativity Research Journal* 16 (4): 361–88.

2004b. "Types of Creativity Training: Approaches and Their Effectiveness." *The Journal of Creative Behavior* 38 (3): 149–79. https://doi.org/10.1002/ j.2162-6057.2004.tb01238.x.

Shanmugam, Ramalingam. 2018. "Elements of Causal Inference: Foundations and Learning Algorithms." *Journal of Statistical Computation and Simulation* 88 (16): 3248–48. https://doi.org/10.1080/00949655.2018.1505197.

Shenefelt, Michael, and Heidi White. 2013. *If A, Then B: How the World Discovered Logic*. New York: Columbia University Press.

Shumailov, Ilia, Zakhar Shumaylov, Yiren Zhao, et al. 2023. "The Curse of Recursion: Training on Generated Data Makes Models Forget." *arXiv Preprint arXiv:2305.17493.*

2024. "AI models collapse when trained on recursively generated data." *Nature* 631, 755–759. https://doi.org/10.1038/s41586-024-07566-y.

Simonton, Dean Keith. 2013. "Creative Thought as Blind Variation and Selective Retention: Why Creativity Is Inversely Related to Sightedness." *Journal of Theoretical and Philosophical Psychology* 33 (4): 253–66. https://doi.org/ 10.1037/a0030705.

2015. "On Praising Convergent Thinking: Creativity as Blind Variation and Selective Retention." *Creativity Research Journal* 27 (3): 262–70. https:// doi.org/10.1080/10400419.2015.1063877.

Simony, Erez, Christopher J. Honey, Janice Chen, et al. 2016. "Dynamic Reconfiguration of the Default Mode Network during Narrative Comprehension." *Nature Communications* 7 (1): 12141. https://doi.org/ 10.1038/ncomms12141.

Sloman, Steven A. 2009. *Causal Models: How People Think about the World and Its Alternatives*. Oxford, UK: Oxford University Press.

Sloman, Steven A., and David Lagnado. 2015. "Causality in Thought." *Annual Review of Psychology* 66 (1): 223–47. https://doi.org/10.1146/annurev-psych-010814-015135.

Sola, Eric, Robert Hoekstra, Stephen Fiore, and Pamela McCauley. 2017. "An Investigation of the State of Creativity and Critical Thinking in Engineering Undergraduates." *Creative Education* 8 (9): 1495–522. https://doi.org/ 10.4236/ce.2017.89105.

Song, Hayoung, Bo-yong Park, Hyunjin Park, and Won Mok Shim. 2021. "Cognitive and Neural State Dynamics of Narrative Comprehension."

Journal of Neuroscience 41 (43): 8972–90. https://doi.org/10.1523/JNEUROSCI.0037-21.2021.

Spearman, Charles. 1920. *The Nature of "Intelligence" and the Principles of Cognition.* London: Macmillan.

——— 1930. *Creative Mind.* Cambridge: Cambridge University Press

Stepin, Ilia, Jose M. Alonso, Alejandro Catala, and Martín Pereira-Fariña. 2021. "A Survey of Contrastive and Counterfactual Explanation Generation Methods for Explainable Artificial Intelligence." *IEEE Access* 9: 11974–12001.

Sternberg, Meir. 1992. "Telling in Time (II): Chronology, Teleology, Narrativity." *Poetics Today* 13 (3): 463–541.

——— 2003. "Universals of Narrative and Their Cognitivist Fortunes (I)." *Poetics Today* 24 (2): 297–395.

Storm, Benjamin C., and Genna Angello. 2010. "Overcoming Fixation: Creative Problem Solving and Retrieval-Induced Forgetting." *Psychological Science* 21 (9): 1263–65. https://doi.org/10.1177/0956797610379864.

Storm, Benjamin C., Annie S. Ditta, and Tim George. 2020. "Memory." In *Encyclopedia of Creativity,* edited by Steven Pritzker, and Mark Runco, 3rd ed., 116–20. Oxford: Academic Press. https://doi.org/10.1016/B978-0-12-809324-5.06232-5.

Strawson, Galen. 2014. *The Secret Connexion: Causation, Realism, and David Hume: Revised Edition.* Oxford, UK: Oxford University Press.

Subramanian, Jyothi, and Richard Simon. 2013. "Overfitting in Prediction Models – Is It a Problem Only in High Dimensions?" *Contemporary Clinical Trials* 36 (2): 636–41.

Summerville, Amy, Brian Kirkmeyer, and Jennifer Blue. 2018. How "What Might Have Been" Can Shape What's Yet to Come: Preliminary Evidence for Counterfactual Thoughts as an Intervention in Early Engineering Courses Paper presented at 2018 ASEE Annual Conference & Exposition, Salt Lake City, Utah. 10.18260/1-2—30098.

Surovek, Andrea E., and Gian Andrea Rassati. 2017. "Is Structural Engineering Education Creating Barriers to Innovation and Creativity." *Proceedings of the 6th Structural Engineers World Congress,* November. https://par.nsf.gov/biblio/10228538-structural-engineering-education-creating-barriers-innovation-creativity.

Swanson, R. N. 1999. *The Twelfth-Century Renaissance.* Manchester: Manchester University Press.

Tampio, Nicholas. 2018. *Common Core: National Education Standards and the Threat to Democracy.* Baltimore, MD: Johns Hopkins University Press.

Tan, Tengteng, Hong Zou, Chuansheng Chen, and Jin Luo. 2015. "Mind Wandering and the Incubation Effect in Insight Problem Solving." *Creativity Research Journal* 27 (4): 375–82. https://widgets.weforum.org/nve-2015/index.html.

Teng, Shan-Chuan, and Yunn-Wen Lien. 2022. "Propensity or Diversity? Investigating How Mind Wandering Influences the Incubation Effect of Creativity." *PLOS ONE* 17 (4): e0267187. https://doi.org/10.1371/journal.pone.0267187.

Tian, Yufei, Abhilasha Ravichander, Lianhui Qin, et al. 2023. "MacGyver: Are Large Language Models Creative Problem Solvers?" *arXiv Preprint arXiv:2311.09682*.

Torrance, E. Paul. 1967. "Understanding the Fourth Grade Slump in Creative Thinking: Final Report." BR-5-0508. Washington, DC: U.S. Department of Health, Education, and Welfare. https://eric.ed.gov/?id=ED018273.

Tsao, J. Y., C. L. Ting, and C. M. Johnson. 2019. "Creative Outcome as Implausible Utility." *Review of General Psychology* 23 (3): 279–92. https://doi.org/10.1177/1089268019857929.

Tsodyks, Misha, Tal Kenet, Amiram Grinvald, and Amos Arieli. 1999. "Linking Spontaneous Activity of Single Cortical Neurons and the Underlying Functional Architecture." *Science* 286 (5446): 1943–46.

Turing, Alan. 1950. "Computing Machinery and Intelligence." *Mind* 59: 433–460. https://doi.org/10.1093/mind/LIX.236.433

Valentine, Andrew, Iouri Belski, and Margaret Hamilton. 2018. "Development of Creativity of Engineering Students: A Cause for Concern?" In *2018 ASEE Annual Conference & Exposition*. https://peer.asee.org/development-of-creativity-of-engineering-students-a-cause-for-concern.

Valentine, Andrew, Iouri Belski, Margaret Hamilton, and Scott Adams. 2019. "Creativity in Electrical Engineering Degree Programs: Where Is the Content?" *IEEE Transactions on Education* 62 (4): 288–96. https://doi.org/10.1109/TE.2019.2912834.

Van Eekelen, Bregje F. 2017. "Creative Intelligence and the Cold War." *Conflict and Society* 3 (1): 92–107. https://doi.org/10.3167/arcs.2017.030108.

Van Hoeck, Nicole, Patrick D. Watson, and Aron K. Barbey. 2015. "Cognitive Neuroscience of Human Counterfactual Reasoning." *Frontiers in Human Neuroscience* (9): 420. https://doi.org/10.3389/fnhum.2015.00420.

Vasconcelos, Luis A., and Nathan Crilly. 2016. "Inspiration and Fixation: Questions, Methods, Findings, and Challenges." *Design Studies* 42 (January): 1–32. https://doi.org/10.1016/j.destud.2015.11.001.

Vinod, Goel, Navarrette Gorka, Ira Noveck, and Jerome Prado. 2017. "The Reasoning Brain: The Interplay between Cognitive Neuroscience and Theories of Reasoning." *Frontiers in Human Neuroscience* 10: 673.

Volchik, Vyacheslav V., and Elena V. Maslyukova. 2018. "The Metrics Trap, or Why Is Implicit Knowledge Underestimated When Regulation of Science and Education Is Handled." *Journal of Institutional Studies* 10 (3): 158–79. https://doi.org/10.17835/2076-6297.2018.10.3.158-179.

Von Neumann, John. 1963. "Various Techniques Used in Connection with Random Digits." *John von Neumann, Collected Works* 5: 768–70.

Vygotsky, Lev. 2004. "Imagination and Creativity in Childhood." *Journal of Russian & East European Psychology* 42 (1): 7–97. https://doi.org/10.1080/10610405.2004.11059210.

Wai, Jonathan, and Joni M. Lakin. 2020. "Finding the Missing Einsteins: Expanding the Breadth of Cognitive and Noncognitive Measures Used in Academic Services." *Contemporary Educational Psychology* 63 (October): 101920. https://doi.org/10.1016/j.cedpsych.2020.101920.

Waismeyer, Anna, and Andrew N. Meltzoff. 2017. "Learning to Make Things Happen: Infants' Observational Learning of Social and Physical Causal Events." *Journal of Experimental Child Psychology* 162 (October): 58–71. https://doi.org/10.1016/j.jecp.2017.04.018.

Walker, Caren M., Sophie Bridgers, and Alison Gopnik. 2016. "The Early Emergence and Puzzling Decline of Relational Reasoning: Effects of Knowledge and Search on Inferring Abstract Concepts." *Cognition* 156 (November): 30–40. https://doi.org/10.1016/j.cognition.2016.07.008.

Walker, Caren M., and Tania Lombrozo. 2017. "Explaining the Moral of the Story." *Cognition* 167 (October): 266–81. https://doi.org/10.1016/j.cognition.2016.11.007.

Wang, Kai, Boxiang Dong, and Junjie Ma. 2019. "Towards Computational Assessment of Idea Novelty." In *Proceedings of the 52nd Hawaii International Conference on System Sciences 2019*. https://doi.org/ISBN:978-0-9981331-2-6, https://ssrn.com/abstract=3393611.

Weinberg, Abraham Itzhak, Cristiano Premebida, and Diego Resende Faria. 2024. "Causality from Bottom to Top: A Survey." *arXiv Preprint arXiv:2403.11219*.

Wente, Adrienne, Alison Gopnik, María Fernández Flecha, Teresa Garcia, and Daphna Buchsbaum. 2022. "Causal Learning, Counterfactual Reasoning and Pretend Play: A Cross-Cultural Comparison of Peruvian, Mixed- and Low-Socioeconomic Status U.S. Children." *Philosophical Transactions of the Royal Society B: Biological Sciences* 377 (1866): 20210345. https://doi.org/10.1098/rstb.2021.0345.

West, Peter, Ximing Lu, Nouha Dziri, et al. 2023. "The Generative AI Paradox: 'What It Can Create, It May Not Understand'." *arXiv e-prints*: arXiv-2311.

Wiggins, Geraint A. 2006a. "A Preliminary Framework for Description, Analysis and Comparison of Creative Systems." *Knowledge-Based Systems, Creative Systems*, 19 (7): 449–58. https://doi.org/10.1016/j.knosys.2006.04.009.

———. 2006b. "Searching for Computational Creativity." *New Generation Computing* 24 (3): 209–22. https://doi.org/10.1007/BF03037332.

———. 2019. "A Framework for Description, Analysis and Comparison of Creative Systems." In *Computational Creativity: The Philosophy and Engineering of Autonomously Creative Systems*, edited by Tony Veale and F. Amilcar Cardoso, 21–47. Cham, Switzerland: Springer.

Wiley, Jennifer. 1998. "Expertise as Mental Set: The Effects of Domain Knowledge in Creative Problem Solving." *Memory & Cognition* 26 (4): 716–30. https://doi.org/10.3758/BF03211392.

Williams, D. L. 2016. "Light and the Evolution of Vision." *Eye* 30: 173–78.

Wong, Matteo. 2024. "Things Get Strange When AI Starts Training Itself." *The Atlantic*, February. www.theatlantic.com/technology/archive/2024/02/artificial-intelligence-self-learning/677484/.

Woodward, James. 2005. *Making Things Happen: A Theory of Causal Explanation*. Oxford Studies in the Philosophy of Science. Oxford, UK: Oxford University Press.

Wu, Zhaofeng, Linlu Qiu, Alexis Ross, et al. 2024. "Reasoning or Reciting? Exploring the Capabilities and Limitations of Language Models Through Counterfactual Tasks." arXiv. https://doi.org/10.48550/arXiv.2307.02477.

Yang, Shiyu, Jeffrey Loewenstein, and Jennifer Mueller. 2023. "Finding Creativity by Changing Perspectives: How the Evaluation Process Contributes to Creative Idea Recognition." *Creativity Research Journal* 35(3): 481–98. https://doi.org/10.1080/10400419.2023.2191900.

Ying, Xue. 2019. "An Overview of Overfitting and Its Solutions." *Journal of Physics: Conference Series* 1168: 022022.

Youmans, Robert J., and Thomaz Arciszewski. 2014. "Design Fixation: Classifications and Modern Methods of Prevention." *Artificial Intelligence for Engineering Design, Analysis and Manufacturing* 28 (2): 129–37. https://doi.org/10.1017/S0890060414000043.

Zečević, Matej, Moritz Willig, Devendra Singh Dhami, and Kristian Kersting. 2023. "Causal Parrots: Large Language Models May Talk Causality but Are Not Causal." *arXiv Preprint arXiv:2308.13067*.

Zenil, Hector. 2011. *Randomness through Computation: Some Answers, More Questions*. Hackensack, NJ: World Scientific.

Zhang, Weitao, Zsuzsika Sjoerds, and Bernhard Hommel. 2020. "Metacontrol of Human Creativity: The Neurocognitive Mechanisms of Convergent and Divergent Thinking." *NeuroImage* 210 (April): 116572. https://doi.org/10.1016/j.neuroimage.2020.116572.

Zhang, Xu-Yao, Cheng-Lin Liu, and Ching Y Suen. 2020. "Towards Robust Pattern Recognition: A Review." *Proceedings of the IEEE* 108 (6): 894–922.

Zhou, Yu, Xingyu Wu, Beicheng Huang, et al. 2024. "CausalBench: A Comprehensive Benchmark for Causal Learning Capability of Large Language Models." *arXiv Preprint arXiv:2404.06349*.

Zhu, Yuxi, Simone M. Ritter, Barbara C. N. Müller, and Ap Dijksterhuis. 2017. "Creativity: Intuitive Processing Outperforms Deliberative Processing in Creative Idea Selection." *Journal of Experimental Social Psychology* 73 (November): 180–88. https://doi.org/10.1016/j.jesp.2017.06.009.

Acknowledgments

The authors would like to express their gratitude for research support and guidance to Pat Enciso, Kelly Wegley, Trent Bowers, Milford Beagle Jr., Lawrence G. Ferguson, David C. Foley, The National Council of Teachers of English, The Ohio State College of Education and Human Ecology, Worthington Schools, The United States Army Nurse Corps, United States Army Special Operations Command, and Army University.

For our students, past and future

Cambridge Elements ≡

Creativity and Imagination

Anna Abraham
University of Georgia, USA

Anna Abraham, Ph.D. is the E. Paul Torrance Professor at the University of Georgia, USA. Her educational and professional training has been within the disciplines of psychology and neuroscience, and she has worked across a diverse range of academic departments and institutions the world over, all of which have informed her cross-cultural and multidisciplinary focus. She has penned numerous publications including the 2018 book, *The Neuroscience of Creativity* (Cambridge University Press), and 2020 edited volume, *The Cambridge Handbook of the Imagination*. Her latest book is *The Creative Brain: Myths and Truths* (2024, MIT Press).

About the Series

Cambridge Elements in Creativity and Imagination publishes original perspectives and insightful reviews of empirical research, methods, theories, or applications in the vast fields of creativity and the imagination. The series is particularly focused on showcasing novel, necessary and neglected perspectives.

Cambridge Elements ≡

Creativity and Imagination

Elements in the Series

A full series listing is available at: www.cambridge.org/ECAI